Love Bade Me Welcome

A British Methodist Perspective on the Church

David Carter

EPWORTH PRESS

British Library Cataloguing in Publication data

A catalogue record for this book is available from
the British Library

0 7162 05572

First published in 2002
by Epworth Press
20 Ivatt Way
Peterborough PE3 7PG

Typeset by Rowland Phototypesetting Ltd,
Bury St Edmunds, Suffolk
and printed in Great Britain by
Creative Print and Design, Wales

Contents

Dedication

This book is dedicated with grateful thanks to Sister Lorelei Fuchs SA, great encourager, and to John Munsey Turner, Pierre Parre and Joseph Florent Famerée, Presbyters in the Church of God.

Acknowledgements

I should like to acknowledge a deep debt of gratitude to many who have, in varying ways, contributed to the making of this book. I begin with the three teachers who first formed me as a historian, Daniel O'Connell, Senior History Master at the Stationers' Company's School, Alec Vidler and John Kent. I thank colleagues and students at Wilson's School and the Open University for their stimulus and support over many years. I thank many in the goodly fellowship of ecumenists for friendship and stimulus: the corporate memberships of the Ecumenical Committees of the Catholic Archdiocese of Southwark and the London SW Methodist District, of the Churches Together Theology and Unity Group, of the British Catholic–Methodist Committee and of the Society for Ecumenical Studies.

Particular thanks are due to Emmanuel Sullivan, Sister Paschal OSB, Martin and Ruth Reardon, Bill Snelson and Bernard Longley for so much encouragement, and, supremely, to the four persons mentioned in the dedication whose kindness, generosity and dedication to good scholarship in the service of the unity of Christ's Church have been quite outstanding. In a sense, John Munsey Turner was at the very beginning and the very end of this book. He it was who, ten years ago, first stimulated my interest in nineteenth-century Methodist theology and ecclesiology. He has also read and commented helpfully upon a draft of this book.

This list of debts is far from exhaustive and I beg forgiveness of those whom space precludes me from mentioning. I acknowledge the clear guidance of my editor, Gerald Burt, and the constant love and patience of my wife, who has so often helped me sort out the mysteries of the computer while she herself has been coping with the enormous demands of ministerial training and probation. In this context, I must also thank David Slight for his expert help. I gratefully acknowledge permission from the Trustees for Methodist Church Purposes to quote from modern Faith and Order documents. Finally, I thank the staff at SCM Press for their helpfulness at each stage.

David Carter

Introduction

Twentieth-century Methodism produced two significant Conference statements on the doctrine of the Church, but, otherwise, relatively little systematic ecclesiology. Some might explain this by arguing that Methodism has never had a developed ecclesiological tradition. They might cite the dictum of Albert Outler in the volume of essays edited by Dow Kirkpatrick in 1964, 'To the question, "is there a Wesleyan ecclesiology?", the answer "yes" says too much, the answer "no" too little.'[1]

They would, however, be wrong to endorse Outler's view uncritically. Whatever may be true of the American Methodist tradition, there can be no doubt that nineteenth-century British Wesleyans developed a strong ecclesiological tradition in the course of defending themselves against Independents and high episcopalians as well as dissident Methodists. Benjamin Gregory also produced his *The Holy Catholic Church*, the Fernley Lecture for 1873 and still, arguably, the greatest, if at times somewhat idiosyncratic, work of Methodist ecclesiology ever produced.[2] James Rigg and others argued persuasively for Methodism as a sound typos or style of Christian life and devotion and for its 'connexional' system as having a rather better basis in the practice of the apostolic Church than rival systems of church government claiming an exclusively apostolic basis.[3]

Unfortunately, much of this heritage has been forgotten. It could be argued that Methodists have overexalted the Wesleys: it can certainly be argued that they have undervalued their successors as theologians.

Others might argue that Methodism has little to contribute

to current ecclesiological debate. They would be betraying their ignorance of the classical Wesleyan heritage in ecclesiology as well as overlooking the significant current interest being shown by discerning ecumenists from our sister churches in connexionalism as an expression of *koinonia* or communion in the Church. Both Mary Tanner, the Anglican, and George Tavard, the Roman Catholic, have called for Methodism to articulate its self-understanding as a contribution to the debate.[4]

Much of the difficulty in articulating Methodist ecclesiology lies in the famous 'society–church' debate. Clearly Methodism began as a religious society. Its founders, the Wesley brothers, wanted it to influence and revitalize the contemporary Church of England. They had no desire to separate from the latter. Naturally, then, they never developed a coherent ecclesiology applicable to their movement and thus a corpus of ecclesiological tradition upon which their successors could build. In any case, John's understanding both of Church and ministry remained in flux till the end of his life.[5]

Even after the death of the Wesleys and the practical separation of Methodism from the Church of England, Methodism in England retained much of the ethos of a society and the term 'Wesleyan Methodist Church' was only adopted as late as 1897.[6] To point to the enduring societary features of Methodism is not, however, to deny a real sense of ecclesial consciousness. As Benjamin Gregory maintained in 1888, the Church is, or should be, a 'society'.[7] Time and time again, the classical Wesleyan ecclesiologists argued that Methodism made full provision, principally through the discipline of the class-meeting, for a fullness of fellowship that had characterized primitive Christianity but which was otherwise lacking in other contemporary churches. If Methodism has lacked a full and formally defined ecclesiology, it cannot be said to have lacked a very distinctive ecclesial consciousness, summed up, as far as ordinary Methodists were and are concerned, in the perennially popular hymns of the Wesleys 'for the Society meeting'.[8]

The aim, then, of this book is to explore the Methodist ecclesiological heritage and to expose its multi-faceted richness for

reflection amid the demands of contemporary mission and ecumenism. It is also intended to stimulate further reflection and
research. In no way do I claim to offer a comprehensive, much
less definitive, treatment of the subject. My concern is primarily
with the British Methodist ecclesiological heritage. Very rarely
shall I touch on American Methodism, while being aware that
that tradition also is badly in need of exploration and of comparative study vis-à-vis the British tradition.[9] I end with a summary of what seem to me to be the enduring core points of
Methodist ecclesiology and an overall reflection on Methodism's
potential contribution to the ecclesiology of the Universal
Church, a matter of particular concern to me as a convinced
and committed ecumenist, and a brief note on developments
since the approval of the report *Called to Love and Praise*
(1999).[10]

I

The Ecclesiological Heritage of the Wesleys and the First Methodists

This chapter aims to explore both the complex and shifting ecclesiology of the Wesleys and that of their earliest associates. It must not be assumed that they were identical. Richard Heitzenrater and others have pointed out that Methodism soon developed a life of its own with aims and desires which did not necessarily accord entirely with those of the Wesley brothers.[1] Within John's lifetime, both the strength of his personality and the real veneration with which he was regarded held back Methodists from pushing their deviating desires to the point of rupture with their leader. What is clear is that, almost from the beginning, the infant societies developed a sense of cohesion and identity that was in some degree of tension with the stated desire of the Wesleys that their movement should remain linked to the Church of England. The Wesleys saw their structures as complementing those of the Church of England and their 'prudential means of grace', such as the class meeting and other Methodist innovations, complementing rather than replacing the spirituality of the *Book of Common Prayer*. They wanted their followers to use all the instituted means of grace and worship available in the local parish church. This ideal, however, was far from realized, sometimes as a result of the intolerance of Anglican incumbents, sometimes as a result of the inclinations of the Methodists themselves, many of whom had no background in Anglican worship. From the beginning, they looked to the worship of the societies and the fellowship of the classes to provide their staple spiritual fare.[2]

The nineteenth-century Wesleyans claimed for Methodism an ecclesial reality and consciousness dating back to its origins. James Rigg argued that the Methodist revival was as much a revival of apostolic church life as of primitive doctrine.[3] He was to claim that the ecclesial structures of Methodism developed both to safeguard the Arminian evangelical experimentalism that he saw as the core of Methodism and in response to the instinctive desire of the faithful to associate for their edification in this faith. He and others saw the rise of Methodism as providential, as unplanned in contrast to the deliberate remodelling of church life at the Reformation, but not on that account any less the work of God; rather, they saw precisely in the ad hoc evolution of Methodism the hand of a providence that could be only that of God. Wesley, himself, had shared this perception. In his *Plain Account of the People Called Methodists* he wrote:

> They had no previous design at all; but everything arose just as the occasion offered. They saw or felt some impending or pressing evil, or some good end necessary to be pursued. And many times they fell unawares on the very thing which secured the good or removed the evil. At other times, they consulted on the most probable means, following only common sense and Scripture.[4]

Rigg and the nineteenth-century Wesleyans had an axe to grind in making such claims for the providential rise of Methodism. Nevertheless, they were right to detect in the movement a new 'typos' or style of Christian community living which made integrated sense to those living it and which was certainly distinct from the style of eighteenth-century Anglicanism in general. They wanted also to show that the split from Anglicanism which happened at the end of the eighteenth century had been implicit and inevitable from the beginning. They argued that, if Wesley had opposed any idea of separation from the Church of England, this was because of residual and regrettable high-church principles that continued to influence him even after his evangelical conversion of 1738.[5]

The natural tendency of Rigg and other Wesleyans was to read back the conditions of their age into the eighteenth century. The situation, despite the very real and distinctive ethos of Methodism, was, however, more complex. Not only the Wesleys balked at the idea of separation but also many of their followers, if only out of loyalty to their leaders' known views. There continued after 1795 and the 'Plan of Pacification' to be 'church' Methodists who not only respected and used the worship of Anglican churches but were also very uneasy about the idea of Methodist preachers administering the sacraments.[6]

Nevertheless, there is evidence that, from at least the 1750s, there were Methodists who wanted the sacraments administered by their own preachers. They wanted a church life separate from Anglicanism. Nor can John Wesley be regarded as failing to contribute to this process. Whatever his hopes for the ultimate compatibility of his societies with Anglican life, he was clearly conscious of a degree of ecclesiological innovation. Thus, he wrote in 1748 that 'we introduce Christian fellowship where it was utterly destroyed'.[7] He was also conscious from an early stage that, under certain circumstances and however reluctantly, he had to break with Anglican rules. Thus he could say that 'Church or no Church, we must attend to the saving of souls'.[8] Whatever Wesley's ambivalence in the matter, many of the Methodist people felt themselves to be a separate people living a different style of Christian life. The Wesley brothers themselves differed in the degree of horror with which they regarded a possible future schism. Charles summed the difference up thus: 'All the difference between my brother and me was that my brother's first object was the Methodists and then the Church; mine was first the Church and then the Methodists.'[9] Perhaps the greatest irony in this situation is that it was Charles Wesley who, albeit presumably totally unconsciously, contributed to the increasing Methodist sense of 'separateness'. His hymns for the Society meeting and parting and his hymns for the love feasts articulated in singable form a new ecclesial consciousness.[10] They encapsulated the sense of the Methodist people, which might otherwise have been less effectively articulated, that they were a truly apostolic Christian community, bearing the same witness and experiencing the same joys and sufferings as the communities described in the New Testament.[11]

Hymn no. 753 in *Hymns and Psalms*, 'All praise to our redeeming Lord', is a hymn that has been perennially popular in Methodism. It articulates a rich ecclesial sense, moving from the initial act of divine grace 'who joins us by His grace' through emphasis upon mutual edification, 'he bids us build each other up', common pilgrimage, 'to our high calling's glorious hope, we hand in hand go on', the circulation of love and experience in verse 3, to unity in joy and peace and anticipation of the Church of the end-time in the last verse. The lyricism of verses 3, 5 and 6, quoted below, contains within itself a whole theology of communion or *koinonia*, to use modern ecumenical jargon.

> The gift that he on one bestows,
> We all delight to prove;
> The grace through every vessel flows,
> In purest streams of love.
>
> We all partake the joy of one,
> The common peace we feel,
> A peace to sensual minds unknown,
> A joy unspeakable.
>
> And if our fellowship below
> In Jesus be so sweet,
> What heights of rapture shall we know
> When round his throne we meet!

The experience of salvation is at one and the same time intensely personal and totally corporate.

Other hymns also testify to the dynamic ecclesial experience of early Methodism. Examples are 'Christ from whom all blessings flow' (*HP* 764) and 'Jesus, Lord, we look to thee' (*HP* 759) with its emphasis on the mutual love and care experienced in the societies as they advanced in the pilgrimage towards holiness and perfect love.

The fact that these three hymns have remained in the succeeding official hymn books of Methodism testifies to a perennial appeal. One may argue that the experience of fellowship in more recent Methodism has lost something of the intensity, and certainly of the self-discipline, of early Methodism, but the sense that these are appropriate ideals of community Christian living has certainly not totally departed. The personal experience of the author, as a local preacher, is that the three hymns cited above are still well known and there is never any difficulty in persuading even the most limited of organists or pianists to play the relevant set tune at services.

It is important to make this point as early as possible in this book. Much of it will be concerned with the insights and theologizing of Methodist scholars. Important as their insights may be, and as deserving of reception or 're-reception' within the current ecumenical ecclesiological debate as may be the case, it is important not to overlook the backdrop of popular Methodist ecclesial awareness against which they worked.

Equally, however, it is important not to overlook the ecclesiology of the Wesleys themselves. John remained, of course, the single most powerful influence on the Methodism of his lifetime, and the construction of his theological thought long remained central to Methodist theological endeavour. However, it is true to say that his complex, and rather shiftingly idiosyncratic ecclesiology, has not yet received adequate attention. Some might argue that the endeavour would be fruitless. Wesley was not a systematic thinker. His theological thinking was constantly changing under the pressure of events. For him Scripture and Tradition were important, but so also were reason and experience. Part of the problem in interpreting him is that Wesley did not move consistently away from an inherited high-Anglican emphasis on the importance of tradition to attitudes based on experience. Rather, the four elements of the Methodist 'quadrilateral', Scripture, reason, Tradition and experience, remained fluidly and variably combined in his thinking and practice.

Wesley might insist that he was a man of one book and that he recognized no authority other than that of Scripture. However, he could also couple the authority of 'common sense' with that of Scripture, as we have already seen.[12] He clearly believed that pragmatic innovation and adaptability were acceptable and legitimate provided they served goals which could ultimately be shown to be scriptural. Thus, in response to criticisms that he was no more than an unprincipled innovator, Wesley wrote: 'But these, said another, are all men's innovations . . . They are methods which men have found, by reason and common sense, for more effectively applying several Scriptural rules, couched in general terms, to particular occasions.'[13]

Interpretation of his legacy was all too easily bedevilled by those propagandists, both within Methodism and in later Anglicanism, who wanted to claim Wesley for their own views. James Rigg and other Victorian Wesleyans believed that Wesley's ecclesiology developed in a logical line, granted the importance of his 'conversion' of 1738. We are no longer so sure of the absolute centrality of that event in May 1738. Rigg argued that, after 1738, Wesley steadily purged himself of the unbiblical and proto-Tractarian views that he had unfortunately imbibed in his youth.[14] Rigg granted that, occasionally, Wesley so forgot himself as temporarily to revert to those views in certain particulars on peculiar occasions. Modern historians do not feel able to endorse Rigg's view nor the opposite view of those Victorian high Anglicans who maintained that Wesley stayed loyal to his early convictions. As far as one can generalize in such a complex matter, it seems that one cannot categorize Wesley's ecclesiology as conforming entirely to any of the patterns that later thinkers wished to impose on it. It was an extraordinary melange of overlapping insights and influences. In recent years, Frank Baker, E. W. Thompson, Frederick Hunter, A. B. Lawson, Colin Williams and Henry Rack have all shed light on the ecclesiological heritage of the Wesleys.[15] Hunter has pointed to the perduring influence of Wesley's early high church notions (which he particularly attributed to non-juror influences between 1732 and 1736), coexisting in tension with later modifications and more

Protestant influences coming at and after the time of his evangelical conversion.[16] Williams argues that three strands of ecclesiological thought coexist in Wesley's ecclesiology, a 'catholic' emphasis on the value of preserving order and continuity where at all possible, a classical Protestant view, which was enshrined within Anglican article 19 (itself an adaptation of Lutheran teaching), which held that the Church existed wherever the word was purely preached and the two gospel sacraments of Baptism and Eucharist were duly administered, and a more 'free church' emphasis on the importance of the gathered congregation of the saints. This last element presumably owed much to the influence of Wesley's Puritan forebears.[17]

Particularly important and instructive for the ecumenical era are Wesley's attempts to hold in tension the importance of historical continuity, as a sign of Christ's continuing faithfulness to his Church, and a contrasting emphasis on a succession of pastors and prophets in the Church whose divine appointment is attested by the success attending their ministry rather than by ecclesiastical pedigree as such. When we look at Wesley's evolving view of the ministry, we find a continuing tension between a more historical/ontological approach and a more functional one. Wesley's liberation, as a result of reading Lord Justice King in 1746, from a rigid view of the absolute necessity of the historic, episcopal succession did not prevent him from preaching the famous sermon on the 'sons of Korah' in 1789. However, the high, sacerdotal doctrine of the presbyterate therein contained was also in tension with his earlier stated view that the end of all ministerial order was the building up of souls in fear and love, something that Wesley clearly believed was achievable through the ministry of his unordained travelling preachers.[18] His action in ordaining for America was undoubtedly a breach of established Anglican discipline, but it is equally noteworthy that he wished to preserve a threefold order of ministry for the new Church as one that was most agreeable to the Scriptures and to the Primitive Church.[19]

The ambiguities of Wesley's doctrine of the ministry, and particularly his understanding of right ministerial order and succession, relate to his wider ecclesiological ambiguities. He always seems to have regarded separation as an evil, an evil that might in certain circumstances become a necessity, but was, nevertheless, to be avoided if at all possible. Thus, he wrote, 'God could have made us separate . . . but that would have been a direct contradiction of his design in raising us up'.[20] His ideal remained that Methodism should be a 'revival' movement within established church structures. Ted Runyon comments, 'Wesley's basic ecclesiology adheres neither to state church nor to sectarian criteria. He intends a genuinely ecumenical renewal movement able to benefit all Christian bodies.'[21] Perhaps the last phrase is stretching the evidence. Wesley was not directly concerned with the state of the small, old-dissenting and Roman Catholic bodies of his time. He was primarily concerned with the Church of England. Nevertheless, in view of his sermon 'On the Catholic Spirit', it is perhaps not a false development of his teaching to argue, as some have done, that the ultimate ecumenical destiny of Methodism is to be once again an order within the Universal Church standing for an approach to mission and holiness that is meant to leaven the whole.[22]

A neglected aspect of Wesley's ecclesiology is his emphasis upon the practically deleterious effects of schism. It is true that he regarded schism, biblically, as relating to disharmony within a church rather than to separation as such. His sermon 'On Schism', nevertheless, regards separation as a 'grievous breach of the law of love' and as productive of 'evil fruits'. He saw clearly that, in a situation of separation, intolerance and mis-understanding would grow. He certainly held that there were situations in which separation had to occur, as when a church clearly departed from Scripture in its practice or teaching, but he was not blind to the evils that could and would then inevitably arise. As he acidly commented, 'the experiment [i.e. of separation] has been so frequently tried already, and the success never answered the expectation'.[23]

Runyon is surely right, however, to point to a tension between more catholic and universal and more 'sectarian' elements in Wesley's ecclesiology. As he points out, Wesley was marked both by early pietism and by reaction against it. He wanted to insist both on the divine institution and the human, voluntary nature of the Church. As Runyon asserts, citing Wesley, God 'fills, pervades and actuates the whole', but, at the same time, the person who does not become and remain an active member of this Church is not a genuine member of it. As Runyon puts it, it is not enough to be baptized; we must live 'answerable to our baptism'. Wesley, however, parts with sectarianism in two respects; first, in his insistence that the Church is not limited to a spiritual elite, but that its fellowship should be open to all who are genuine seekers after salvation; secondly, and perhaps even more importantly, in his sense that the Church has both a continuing mission to its errant members and a wider role vis-à-vis the whole of humankind. Thus we find Wesley saying that 'in some sense it is the mother of us who have been brought up therein' and also that 'God has so mingled you together with other men that whatever grace you have received of God may through you be communicated to others'. Methodism has a breadth of missionary orientation that eclipses that of a mere sect.[24]

Methodists are still exploring the ecclesiology implicit in Wesley's actions as well as that which can be directly evidenced from the sermons and tracts. David Lowes Watson, in a study of early Methodist class meetings, has argued that the key feature of Wesleyan ecclesiology was an emphasis on 'mutual accountability'. In the class meeting, the most basic, intimate unit for Christian fellowship, Methodists week by week gave account of their progress in grace and discipleship, an account that was meant to edify all members of the group. In the class meeting, experiences, joyous, painful and salutary alike, were all meant to be shared in order that others might, as appropriate, be encouraged, warned or enlightened by them.[25]

Looking at Methodism on a more global level, the Singaporean Methodist scholar R. George Eli argues that Methodist discipleship and ecclesial practice were dominated by the missiological aim of 'social holiness', of indicating to the world, through the example of the grace-transformed life of their own

communities, the potential for transformation of social relationships through the power of God. According to Eli, the Methodist
concept and practice of discipleship 'involved the process of
nurturing the Christian life through redeemed community, a
process through which redeemed community also reached out
in social holiness to the world'. Eli considers that Methodist
experience was inescapably ecclesial and that any subsequent
tendency in Methodism to pietistic individualism represents a
betrayal of the true tradition, Wesley having repudiated mysti-
cism, quietism and Moravianism on account of such tendencies.
He emphasized the role of the experience of God's grace in
building up 'graced communities, bound not by specific rules of
conduct, positive or negative, but by a limitless concern for the
advancement of God's kingdom'. Eli's contrast, with its appar-
ent disparagement of rules, here may be questioned. The disciplined life of Methodism, the walking by rule that it commended
was meant to encourage not to restrict 'limitless concern'. Wesley's own teaching was that 'the New Testament knows no
holiness but social holiness'.

Eli's interpretation can be questioned. Perhaps it savours too
much of a reading back into Wesley of what the author wishes
to be the case for the sake of current apologetics. R. W. Dale
held that Wesley's view of holiness never really extended to
social righteousness. He drove too hard a wedge between the
sacred and secular.[26]

'As a corporate structure, Methodist community functioned
as an organised unit with the singular goal of serving Christ in
order to transform society.' Eli asserts that this was linked to Wesley's Arminian optimism and belief in the potential sanctification
of all. 'Wesley's unique claim is that God's grace has no limits in
human experience, so that even the poorest illiterate may, through
redemption, find new hope, new possibilities and a new future in
life.'[27] Eli relates this emphasis to Wesley's repeated teaching on
the role of Christians as 'salt' and 'light' in the world and to his
very real belief that the kingdom was destined for this world
and not simply for the next. He cites Wesley's 'Notes on the
New Testament' on Matthew 5.3 and 5.10.

The kingdom of God and the kingdom of heaven ... mean not barely a future happy state in heaven, but a state to be enjoyed on earth ... It properly signifies here, the gospel dispensation, in which subjects were to be gathered to God by his Son, and a society to be formed, which was to subsist first on earth, and afterwards with God in Glory.

May Thy kingdom come quickly, and swallow up all the kingdoms of the earth. May all mankind, receiving Thee, O Christ ... be filled with righteousness, and peace and joy ... till they are all removed hence into thy kingdom of glory, to reign with thee for ever and ever.[28]

Eli asserts that in his discourses on the Sermon on the Mount, Wesley teaches that: 'God commissions the Christian community to attest to God's love and grace in the life of this community and to announce to all persons and societies that such love and grace can be theirs also.' Eli places his assessment of Wesley's transformative and missiological approach to ecclesiology in the widest possible theological perspective. 'Grace creates responsible discipleship, enabling redeemed persons to be response-able, i.e., capable of responding.'[29] This characteristic of responsibility reflects the accountability that God demands of all human society as his creation. 'Christian community is made self-critical by such accountability, and is critical of society by virtue of the responsibility that accrues to such accountability.' One may see this statement of Eli's also as a useful gloss on the modern ecumenical acknowledgement that the Church is 'sign and fore-taste of the Kingdom'. Eli has done a useful job in pointing to an important implicit aspect of Wesley's ecclesiology that tunes in with so much of the modern ecumenical ecclesiological quest.[30] He has shown us that Wesley's concepts of mission and holiness are inescapably ecclesial.

Wesley was influenced by reason and experience, notably by the experience of others. He was fond, after 1746, of asserting that the New Testament prescribed no one form of church government or ministry. In the conferences of 1745 and 1746, Wesley advanced some rather speculative opinions, in the true spirit of the Enlightenment, as to the origin and development of church government, which he saw as a series of natural, but not, per se, God-ordained developments. He also commented on the diversity of order witnessed to in the New Testament, arguing that, without doubt, 'the wisdom of God had a regard to this necessary variety'.[31] In this latter opinion he was to be faithfully followed by his successors in Methodism. Both Wesley and his nineteenth-century successors believed that the Spirit left the sorting out of forms of ministry and organization to the good sense and adaptability of the apostles and later leaders. Different times and places might well demand different forms of church order. This point has not perhaps received the reflection, either within or beyond Methodism, that it deserves.[32]

The shifting sands of Wesleyan ecclesiology are made even more difficult to negotiate by the complex question of Wesley's precise aims. We have already indicated that, at the beginning of the Revival, Wesley had no intention whatsoever of forming a separate church. Rather, he hoped to revitalize the Church of England through the 'gingering up' effect of his societies and his preachers, the latter being described by him as 'extraordinary mesengers, designed of God to provoke others to jealousy'.[33] The trouble was that, in the main, they provoked to antagonism rather than emulation, and in this, and the inevitable reaction to it, came the seeds of future schism, a schism that John Wesley continued to the end to hope to avoid, while perhaps reckoning with the ultimate inevitability of it after his death. Charles was filled with horror at the prospect and strained every muscle to dissuade his brother from any compromising action.[34] Both men must have felt the tension between the type of life emerging in the societies that Charles encapsulated in so many of his hymns on personal and ecclesial Christian experience and the normal life of the contemporary Church of England. Yet despite their extolling of the apostolic primitive purity of the life of Methodism, neither brother was a primitive 'restorationist' believing that they either could or should replicate the exact conditions of primitive Christianity.[35] They had too great a respect for the continuing fecundity of tradition and too great a 'catholic' sense of the diversity of the Church and the enrichment brought to it across many generations. John also had a great sense of the continuing work of providence within his movement. Methodism had been raised up to spread 'Scriptural holiness' through out the land. The success of the lay preachers in this convinced Wesley of the 'lawfulness of the proceeding'.[36] To the centrality of love and holiness, Wesley was prepared to subordinate almost anything, but not in a manner that implied indifference: he did not regard all ways, all means, as equally satisfactory. Though he would certainly, at least from the late 1740s have regarded ecclesiological differences, in terms of ministerial order, as matters of 'opinion' rather than central, non-negotiable doctrinal fact, he would not have regarded them as indifferent, as his sermon on the Catholic spirit clearly shows.[37]

With all this fluidity to take into account, what can we say is central to Wesleyan ecclesiology? I think that, despite the caveats entered, we can categorize its main characteristics as follows. It was primitivist, non-exclusivist and connexional. Finally, it placed great emphasis upon the role of carefully administered oversight linked to a clear scheme of ecclesiastical discipline.

We begin with Wesley's 'primitivism'. I use this term deliberately, since, as has already been said, 'restorationism', in terms of any attempt to replicate the exact pattern of primitive Church life, has never been a feature of Methodism at any stage. What Wesley desired was that the ardor and dedication of the apostolic age and the patristic era should again characterize the life of the Church of God. Wesley's reverence for the Church of the first three centuries was not primarily on account of its theological achievement. Rather, it was due to his respect for its purity of life and love. A sermon of 1777 sums up his approach.

Methodism, so called, is the old religion, the religion of the Bible, the religion of the primitive Church, the religion of the Church of England [it is interesting to note Wesley's emphasis on the two latter points, always central to his apologetic against his detractors in the Church of England]. It is none

other than the love of God, the love of all mankind ... This
religion of love, and joy and peace has its seat in the inmost
soul; but ever showing itself by its fruits, constantly springing
up. This is the religion of the Bible ... this is the religion of
the primitive Church, the whole Church in the purest ages.
It is clearly expressed and even in the fourth century, it is
found in the works of Gregory, Basil, Ephraim Syrus and
Macarius.[38]

Wesley, characteristically, here links an emphasis on the solidly
biblical basis of such religion with its constant lively exemplifi-
cation and experience in the later ages of the Church. It is the
truly 'catholic' experience across time and space, of the 'faith
that sweetly works by love' to quote his brother Charles.[39] Lest,
however, it be thought that Wesley's emphasis on experience
and practice led him to devalue order as such, one must balance
this overriding emphasis, to a degree, with that found in sermon
104, 'On Attending the Church Service', where Wesley insists,
against the developing prejudices of some early Methodists, that
the sacraments conveyed grace even when administered by
unworthy men. 'Their efficacy derives not from him that admin-
isters but from Him who ordains it.' With Wesley, there is a
fine balance between what is historic, ordered and covenanted
and what is providentially, pneumatically and 'irregularly
bestowed'.[40] This enabled him to affirm both the reality and
abiding significance of the 'covenanted means of grace', specified
in Scripture and practised universally in the Church, and the
'prudential means', arising from within particular traditions at
particular times. Wesley's views were broader than both those
of 'traditionalist' Catholics and than those of many Protestants
reacting against them. It was extremely difficult for Methodism
to maintain the founder's nuanced and genuinely 'catholic'
appreciation after his death, an appreciation that has only resur-
faced in some quarters in modern Methodism as a result both
of intensified study of Wesley and of ecumenical influences.[41]
   The second key emphasis in Wesley's ecclesiology was that
of a generous inclusivity. While he continued to his dying day

to esteem the Church of England as the most scriptural of all churches, he came to an increasing appreciation of others. By 1747, he acknowledged the ecclesial reality of continental Reformed churches in a way that he would never have done in his youth. At the Conference of that year, he said, 'it would be a consequence full of shocking absurdity' to hold that 'they are no parts of the Church of Christ'.[42] His appreciation of others was always balanced with a candid assessment of their defects as he saw them. Thus, he could express great admiration of the Counter-Reformation and later saints of Rome while candidly criticizing the superstition that seemed to him so endemic in the Roman system as he, rather imperfectly, knew it. His view of Rome was, typically, not a stable one and the Wesley of the 'Letter to a Roman Catholic', in 1749, was much more eirenic than the Wesley of 1778 with his opposition to the degree of Catholic emancipation then conceded by law.[43]

Wesley changed his mind on the necessity of the historic episcopate in 1746, but he never ceased to regard 'episkope', or oversight, as essential to the Church. He deprecated the effective lack of exercise of true episkope by the Anglican bishops of his day. 'Who watched over them in faith and love? Who marked their growth in grace?'[44] He was as insistent as any Calvinist on the importance of an effective ministry of episkope at the most local level, hence the authority entrusted to the preachers who were 'to mind every point of our discipline' and enforce it with the assistance of the class-leaders, over whose subordinate role the preachers were to keep a constant watching brief. Wesley's emphasis, however, differed from that of Calvinism in its more positive tone. Episcope was not merely to be negatively disciplinary; it was to be encouraging, promoting real growth in holiness, as denoted in the question, 'Who marked their growth in grace?' This marked off the Wesleyan concept of episkope from the more limited one prevailing in the contemporary Reformed churches. Wesley's emphasis upon the importance of episkope was reinforced by his own profound sense of the providential origin and development of Methodism. He justified the very personal episkope that he exercised over the Connexion throughout his lifetime by citing the providential way in which the movement, without deliberate planning on his part, had developed. When chided for the way in which he monopolized decision making he replied:

> I myself sent for these [i.e. the travelling preachers whom he called to the Conference] of my own free choice; and I sent for them to advise, not to govern me. Neither did I, at any of those times, divest myself of any part of that power described, which the Providence of God had cast upon me, without any design or choice of mine.[45]

Wesley believed that the very precise rules and discipline which he exerted, in conjunction with the travelling preachers working strictly at his direction, were necessary to the cohesion of the movement and to its central aim of 'spreading Scriptural holiness'. He did not deny that there could be other legitimate forms of discipline within the Church. He believed that Christians had the right to choose under which pastors they should place themselves for the good of their souls. However, he also believed that they then contracted a duty of obedience to those pastors. Both he and later Wesleyans frequently justified this duty by citing Hebrews 13.17: 'Obey the pastors that are set over you'. Never should Christians attempt to disrupt the life of a church by stirring up internal antagonism against its lawful pastors and its disciplinary system.[46]

The emphasis upon episkope 'from above', by Wesley or his preachers, should not blind us to a parallel emphasis upon mutual oversight within the societies, classes and bands. This appears clearly in the minutes of the Conference for 1748, where the vital necessity of the societies is stressed. 'They cannot watch over one another in love unless they are thus united together. Nor (3) can believers build one another up and bear one another's burthens.' It is almost as though Wesley anticipated the modern emphasis, within a theology of *koinonia*, upon episkope as personal, collegial and communal.[47]

As far as fully constituted churches were concerned, Wesley

came, by 1761, to believe that true pastors were known by their fruits. The manner of their ordination, whether episcopal or otherwise, was strictly subsidiary to their effectiveness. He said of the pastors of continental Reformed churches: 'they convert sinners to God and none can do so unless God appoint them thereto and assist them therein'.[48] As far as his own practice in conferring pastoral authority was concerned, Wesley was cautious in his claims and his practice. He acknowledged the irregularity of his travelling preachers. He did not ordain them or permit them to preside at the sacraments, despite some pressure on him from the 1760s.[49] It could be argued that the logic of Wesley's evolving position on recognition of ministries by their fruits, and his own practice in only receiving preachers into full connexion when it was established that they had 'fruit to their labours', indicated a pragmatic recognition of his preachers as fully ministerial. Nevertheless, he did not wish a break either with the Church of England or with his brother. He wished his people to receive the sacraments at the hands of the regular Anglican clergy. Effectively, however, Wesley was encouraging a form of dual ecclesial belonging. Given the tension between most of the clergy and Methodism, this dual belonging was likely to prove unstable. Wesley was effectively compartmentalizing church life and attempting to divide it between two bodies, with Methodists looking to the travelling and other Methodist preachers for preaching, instruction and spiritual oversight and to Anglican clergy for the sacraments. This daring piece of ecclesiological innovation and 'dual belonging' could only have persisted had there been great goodwill on both sides.

It could, however, be argued that, in separating the functions of preaching and oversight which he was prepared to concede to his unordained assistants from those of sacramental presidency, Wesley was doing something very curious in terms of Christian tradition. Catholics and Orthodox, on the one hand, and Protestants, on the other, may disagree as to whether presbyteral ordination can be properly conferred by persons other than bishops 'in the historic succession', but generally it is agreed in all three traditions that there is a link between the triple functions of authoritative teaching, sacramental presidency and oversight of a local congregation.

The fourth characteristic of Wesley's ecclesiology was 'connexionalism'. Though the origins of this concept were purely societal, and linked with Wesley's understanding of his own, overall, presiding episkope, there is no doubt that connexionalism was deeply linked to the missionary nature and organization of the societies and to their Arminian theological convictions and eschatological orientation. It has taken Methodism a couple of centuries since the death of the Wesleys to realize that connexionalism is not simply a Methodist 'peculiar institution', or even the ecclesiological consequence of a particular typos of Christian life, but is a valid ecclesiological principle in itself, directly relevant to the Church's institutional expression of its interdependent nature.[50] Its development, like much else in the earliest decades of Methodism, was unpremeditated, but that did not prevent it from subserving vital missionary aims and giving expression to the degree of interdependence that characterized Methodist life. Connexionalism corresponded to the deepest spiritual instincts of Methodism. The ethos of Methodism was very far from purely individualistic, despite the emphasis upon conversion. To the emphasis upon personal responsibility, Wesley and his followers added a 'collective approach', an approach that Rack notes as in stark contrast to the parochialism and congregationalism of the rest of English Protestant Christianity.[51] The Methodists were to be one people, with one mission, that mission itself giving priority not to 'those who want you, but those who want you most'.[52] Methodism was able to achieve a unique degree of penetration of a diverse country. Intense as was the sense of fellowship within each local Methodist society, it was never in danger of seeing itself as the secluded congregation of the saints as was the temptation for many Baptists and Congregationalists. Rather, each society saw its intensity of communal experience of the renewing and transforming grace of God as the manifestation of the one Church of Pentecost within its community, an experience that they knew to be replicated in all other Methodist societies since the

Methodists were 'one people the world over'. It was for Charles Wesley to articulate this sense in hymnody and for later theologians to articulate it in more precise theological terms, but the sense of providential interconnectedness emerged out of the symbiosis of Wesley's skill in developing new and flexible forms of interdependent church life and the experience of communal spiritual renewal that developed within these interdependent communities.

The hymns of Charles Wesley eloquently articulated the Methodist sense of being a true community in *koinonia* in direct replication of the essentials of apostolic experience. Ted Campbell's study, *John Wesley and Christian Antiquity*, shows Wesley as particularly interested in the life and practice, as opposed to specific doctrine, of the Christians of the first three centuries.[53] Charles also sang their faithfulness and their eschatologically charged ardour, as in these lines:

> Come and let us sweetly join
> Christ to praise in hymns divine;
> Give we all with one accord,
> Glory to our common Lord.
>
> Hands and hearts and voices raise:
> Sing as in the ancient days:
> Antedate the joys above,
> Celebrate the feast of love.
>
> Strive we, in affection strive:
> Let the purer flame revive,
> Such as in the martyrs glowed,
> Dying champions for their God.
>
> We, like them, may live and love:
> Called we are their joys to prove,
> Saved with them from future wrath,
> Partners of like precious faith.

> Sing we then in Jesu's name,
> Now as yesterday the same;
> One in every time and place,
> Full for all of truth and grace.[54]

In these lines we see a strong expression of the communion or *koinonia* of the Church across time, a sense, especially, of participation in the same joys and trials, a common sense of eschatological expectancy and a very real belief that the depth and experience of the apostolic age can become real for Christians in every age.

Another couple of verses capture Charles's understanding of the life of the apostolic Church:

> Meek, simple followers of the Lamb,
> With grace abundantly endued,
> A pure, believing multitude,
> They all were of one heart and soul,
> And only love inspired the whole.
>
> O what an age of golden days!
> O what a choice peculiar race!
> Washed in the Lamb's all-cleansing blood,
> Anointed kings and priests to God.[55]

Other hymns of Charles's, no longer familiar to Methodists, catch a heightened awareness of the triumphant pilgrimage of the Methodist people and their awareness of already living, proleptically, in the age to come. We may instance this verse:

> By faith we are come
> To our permanent home:
> By hope we the rapture improve:
> By love we still rise,
> And look down from the skies,
> For the heaven of heavens is love.[56]

In another hymn, no longer sung in contemporary Methodism, we have a delicate balance preserved between the Church's consciousness that, in this world, it has to share the kenotic life of Christ, while simultaneously sharing, mystically, in his exaltation.

> Never let the world break in,
> Fix a mighty gulf between:
> Keep us humble and unknown,
> Prized and loved by God alone.
> Let us still to Thee look up,
> Thee, Thy Israel's strength and hope:
> Nothing know or seek beside
> Jesus and Him crucified.
>
> Dignified with worth divine,
> Let us in thine image shine,
> High in heavenly places sit,
> See the moon beneath our feet,
> Far above created things,
> Look we down on earthly kings,
> Taste our glorious liberty,
> Find our happy all in Thee.[57]

The strongest ecclesiological motif in Charles's hymns is that of dynamic *koinonia*. The life of the Trinity, most especially of the Holy Spirit, suffuses the life of the Church. It is not simply a matter of

> Move and actuate and guide:
> Divers gifts to each divide[58]

but of the fullness of Trinitarian life filling the whole of the Church.

> The gift that he on one bestows,
> We all delight to prove:
> The grace through every vessel flows,
> In purest streams of love.[59]

There is a delightful ambiguity about this verse. Does it relate primarily to the 'sensus fidelium', discerning the authenticity of gifts given to individuals, or does it relate to the process whereby the experience of particular converts becomes the blessed possession and experience of the whole Body? Certainly Methodist worship is characterized by constant epiclesis or invocation of the Spirit upon the whole people of God, that they may time and time again experience the very heights and depths of redeeming grace. Again, we may instance just one verse:

> Send us the Spirit of Thy Son,
> To make the depths of Godhead known,
> To make us share the life divine;
> Send Him the sprinkled blood to apply,
> Send Him our souls to sanctify,
> And show and seal us ever Thine.[60]

The very community, in the unanimity of its supernatural common awareness and agreement concerning the things of God, has its origins in the 'lodestone' of the divine love, the 'attracting sign', as Charles calls it elsewhere.

> Touched by the lodestone of Thy love,
> Let all our hearts agree,
> And ever toward each other move,
> And ever move toward Thee.[61]

James Rigg, commenting upon Acts 2.42–7, talks of the way in which the first Christians instinctively gathered together, not in response to a divine command as such, but because of an implicit instinct for mutual fellowship. Within Charles's hymns, there is a whole dynamic ecclesiology, orientated towards the achievement of unity in holiness. This is particularly evident in the third verse of the hymn, 'Thou God of truth and Love':

> Didst Thou not make us one,
> That we might one remain,
> Together travel on,
> And bear each other's pain:
> Till all Thy utmost goodness prove,
> And rise renewed in perfect love.[62]

The implication of the last couplet is that the achievement and experience of perfect love is an inescapably ecclesial process. The mutuality of growth in grace is also stressed in this verse:

> Help us to help each other Lord,
> Our little stock improve,
> Increase our faith, confirm our hope,
> And perfect us in love.[63]

A final aspect of the Wesleys' ecclesiology remains to be examined: its 'proto-ecumenical' nature. It can best be summed up in the last verse of the hymn 'Christ from whom all blessings flow':

> Love, like death, hath all destroyed,
> Rendered all distinctions void;
> Names and sects and parties fall,
> Thou, O Christ, art all in all.[64]

The Wesleys combined a breadth of recognition of different ecclesial traditions with an understanding that the matters over which they differed were not necessarily matters of indifference. John Wesley could say of the Roman Catholic Church that he could cope with its superstitions, 'yea, even gross superstition', on account of the signal holiness manifested in the lives of so many Catholic saints.[65] In his famous sermon on the 'Catholic Spirit', he acknowledged that fellowship between Christians of widely differing styles of life and churchmanship was desirable, while arguing that not all the 'opinions' over which they differed were necessarily matters of indifference; rather, some opinions were arguably 'better' than others. As in many other matters, John Wesley was not necessarily consistent. Thus, his attitude towards Rome was frequently far from eirenic. His respect for sanctity within the Roman Catholic Church did not stop him issuing numerous tracts designed to convert Roman Catholics.[66] Nor were Charles and John always at one. Charles, despite his verse just quoted, always remained the more rigid Anglican in his attitude to church discipline. However, there was no doubt that the Wesleys, by the standards of their times, espoused a remarkably eirenic attitude towards other Christian traditions and encouraged their followers in making a clear distinction between those things that they regarded as absolutely fundamental and central and those that they regarded as secondary and not warranting any interruption of friendly relationships. Once again, a sense of the prodigal generosity of God's love and the many ways of his providential working through so many situations and ecclesial cultures contributed to this emphasis.

Even taking into account the rich insights of modern Wesley scholarship, it is not easy to summarize the ecclesiological heritage of the Wesleys and of early Methodism. In the thought and practice of the former, classical, pragmatic and experiential strands were all intermingled. The Wesley brothers were heirs to a rich and complex mixture of thought and practice that included elements from both the high Anglican and classical Protestant positions. As their own, largely unpremeditated experiments unfolded, they justified them in terms of their results. John Wesley came to the conclusion that the end of all ministerial order was the salvation of souls.[67] This conclusion did not, however, lead him to see his own experiments in raising up an order of itinerant preachers as necessarily invalidating his previously held view that the threefold ministry of bishop, priest and deacon was normative and to be held to wherever possible. Wesley endeavoured to hold these views in tension. Perhaps this holds a lesson for contemporary Methodism as it contemplates invitations from Anglicans and other episcopally ordered churches to consider adopting 'the sign of the episcopal succession'. At the same time, Methodism insists that it should not 'unchurch' either itself or other non-episcopal churches. Perhaps Methodism can receive 'the sign of the episcopal succession' while insisting that its absence elsewhere does not invalidate a claim to true churchliness where it is obvious that other ministries, however 'extraordinary', to use Wesley's own term, exercise the key functions of authentic Christian teaching and oversight. The key to this ecumenical conundrum may be, as I suggest later on, to balance as complementary, rather than contradictory, doctrines of apostolic 'succession' and 'apostolic recognition'.[68]

As far as the legacy of the wider Methodist movement is concerned, it is one of the 'spreading flame', of recognition that Christian experience is inescapably ecclesial at all levels from the most intensely local and intimate, that is, the class meeting, through to the national and global. That experience is inescapably 'connexional'. It involves those who enter it in a network of relationships at every level, in which they recognize that they are 'one people the world over', because God has called them into one and the same fellowship, in which, ultimately they are all co-responsible, each for all and all for each.

Many issues, of course, remained for the Methodist people to work through. These will be the subject of the following chapters but, for the moment, we need to refer to the most immediate one in order to set the scene for the next chapter. As Wesley moved into his eighties, decisions about the future of Methodism became necessary. How was it to be run after his death? At one point, Wesley had thought of designating the younger Fletcher of Madeley as his successor, but Fletcher's death made that solution impossible. In 1784, Wesley made two decisions relating to the future of Methodism on both sides of the Atlantic. For America, he took a decision that was a clear breach with Anglican order. He ordained Thomas Coke as 'superintendent' for the American work. Wesley felt that he was creating a new church where none had existed beforehand, and that it was necessary for him, a simple presbyter, to do so, since no one else was making the requisite provision. He intended, as he put it, to leave the American brethren to 'the Scriptures and the Primitive Church'. Charles indignantly attacked his brother's action.[69] For Britain, Wesley executed a deed in Chancery, appointing a hundred of the most senior preachers as the Legal Conference, to succeed corporately to his directing authority on his death. Unlike his action in ordaining Coke as superintendent for America, this did not imply a breach with Anglican order in itself, though it did clearly imply that Wesley believed his movement should continue. Granted the feeling of many Methodists it might also be held to imply that he expected the movement to develop an ecclesial life of its own.[70] By the 1790s, the ethos of Methodism had come to differ radically from that of the contemporary Church of England. There was much mutual incomprehension. In the mid-1790s the decisive steps leading to separation were taken. In the process, both churches lost something and elements of bitterness crept into their relationship as Wesley had foreseen.[71]

2

Classical Wesleyan Ecclesiology

In the century following the death of the Wesleys, Methodist apologists developed, first, a general defence of the movement, then, a more sophisticated ecclesiology. That ecclesiology was refined in controversy and debate with the Tractarians, with non-Wesleyan Methodists, all of whom dissented from some aspects of Wesleyan ecclesiology, and with 'Independent' critics. The latter two groups particularly contested the Wesleyan understanding of the place of the ordained ministry, the 'Pastoral Office', within the Church.[1]

A brief account of Methodist history in this period is necessary to set the scene for understanding the ecclesiological issues.[2] In the 1790s, Methodism finally became an independent ecclesial movement. Under the Plan of Pacification of 1795, the travelling preachers could administer the sacraments where the people and the majority of the trustees so desired. Though some Methodists certainly continued to hope for reconciliation with the Church of England and many continued to avail themselves, at least occasionally, of the services of the parish church, Methodism developed more and more of a life of its own. It also grew very rapidly. The membership of the Wesleyan Methodist connexion in 1791 was about 70,000. By the 1840s it had more than quintupled, keeping ahead of natural population increase which more than doubled during the same period. At the same time, other Methodist connexions appeared, of which the Primitive Methodists became the largest and most numerous. In his study, *Jabez Bunting, the Last Wesleyan*, John Kent gives a succinct account of Methodism during the first half of the nineteenth century. He points to the emergence of two styles of Methodism, the 'high' Methodism of the Wesleyan Conference and the 'low Methodism' that characterized the non-Wesleyan groups, but also expressed the mind and sentiments of many 'grass-roots' Wesleyans.[3]

The travelling preachers of Wesley's time inherited a strong *esprit de corps*, fostered by their common discipline which, as has often been pointed out, had much in common with that of a monastic order. Most of them felt a sacred duty to maintain the principles established by Mr Wesley. They certainly shared his view that firm oversight was essential for growth in grace. They feared newer techniques of evangelism which, they felt, ignored the need for orderly 'follow-up' of new converts through disciplined meeting in class and society. To them rapid growth without adequate consolidation was dangerous.

'Low Methodists' read the situation differently. They regarded the Wesleyan establishment as over-cautious and as traitorously abandoning what they saw as Wesley's own adventurous tradition of evangelism. Moreover, they believed in local initiative. They saw their societies flourishing as a result of local activity by class leaders, local preachers and others. They increasingly resented what they saw as the intrusive authority of travelling preachers who were come one year and gone the next, or, at the very least, within three years. The result was the development of a series of secessions from the parent connexion, beginning with the Methodist New Connexion of 1797, and the rise of two important imitative movements, the Primitive Methodists and the Bible Christians, dating from the first two decades of the new century. Their principles and ecclesiology will be considered later in this chapter.

In the earliest years of the nineteenth century, Wesleyan apologists, such as Joseph Benson, were concerned to defend the authenticity of Methodism as a genuine revival of primitive Christianity. They said little directly and specifically about ecclesiology.[4] This reflected the fact that, despite their separation from the Church of England, the Wesleyan leadership still saw their movement more as a Christian society on a large scale rather than as a church, at least not as a church with a very specific identity in contradistinction to others. The 'Establishment' within Wesleyan Methodism cherished sentiments of respect, even at times warmth, towards the Church of England, the 'old Church' as they often called it. They deprecated attacks on its established status and made it clear that, however defective they might regard some of its ministers as being in practice, they accepted its liturgy and doctrine as sound and its system of church government as legitimate.[5]

The retention, for almost all of the nineteenth century, of the language of a society, has bedevilled the discussion of Methodist ecclesiology during this period. The fact that the term 'Wesleyan Methodist Church' was not employed officially until 1897 is misleading as an indicator of ecclesial consciousness, as also is the fact that, in some areas, for a generation and more, Wesleyans continued to attend the parish church, especially to receive the sacraments. Both facts obscure the reality that, whether or not they were in the practice of attending Anglican services and sacraments, the vast majority of Wesleyans enjoyed a distinctive and rich experience of 'church' through their membership of the societies and the class meetings. The interconnected 'connexional' nature of Methodism gave a wider dimension to this belonging and, from early in the century, one can find Wesleyan apologists arguing that Methodists had both a wider and more intense sense of belonging than was characteristic of other denominations. Benjamin Gregory argued that the distinction between 'church' and 'society' represented, in any case, a false dichotomy. According to him, in Methodism, membership of the Church was 'membership of one another'. He continued:

> we are often represented as no longer a society but a Church ... the Church is essentially a society ... in proportion as Methodists drift away from the societary structure of primitive Christianity and Methodism, they inevitably decline from the high Scriptural church standards.[6]

From the 1830s, the earlier kindly regard for the Church of England waned. The Fathers of the Oxford Movement disputed

the very claim of Methodism to authenticity as a Christian movement, let alone as a church in the full sense of the word.[7] Wesleyan Methodism was growing rapidly and becoming much
more tightly structured under the aegis of Jabez Bunting and
others. It was becoming much more self-consciously aware of
itself as a separate ecclesial body, likely to remain as such for an
indefinite future. At the same time, the tensions referred to briefly
above were building up within Methodism. Both imitative movements, such as the Primitive and Independent Methodists, and
directly dissident movements, such as the Protestant Methodists
and the Wesleyan Association, disputed the implicit ecclesiology
and the explicit doctrine of the ministry within Wesleyan
Methodism. At the heart of the disputes were two different concepts of the ministry and of the relationship between the local
congregation and the wider Church. The Wesleyan concept of
the 'Pastoral Office' developed from Wesley's very strong sense
of the need for a ministry that 'watched over' the people 'in
faith and love'. The non-Wesleyan view of the ministry saw it
more purely as an evangelistic agency, used by the churches
rather than governing them. There was also a conflict between
more local and more connexional concepts of church. There is
no doubt that, for many Methodist layfolk, the key immediate
reality was the local church. The pastoral role of the class leader
was seen as more significant than that of the itinerant preacher
whose stay in any one circuit never exceeded three years. The
tensions were compounded by the tactlessness of many itinerant
preachers in their exercise of authority and their 'bending' of
rules to maintain what they saw as their necessary, God-given
authority. Rules adopted by the Conference in 1795 and 1797
to regulate the exercise of authority as between ministers and
the local leaders, particularly the class leaders, were capable of
more than one interpretation. Inevitably, positions could
become polarized. At the same time, 'Independents', most especially Congregationalists, increasingly weighed in to the ecclesiological debate, arguing that the Wesleyan doctrine of the ministry
and connexional ecclesiology both offended against what they
regarded as the New Testament principle of independency.[8]

Out of this maelstrom of controversy, a series of Wesleyan ministers developed a more coherent ecclesiology. Foremost among the earlier apologists were Thomas Jackson (1783–1873), who wrote innumerable pamphlets in support of the Wesleyan understanding of the 'Pastoral Office',[9] and Alfred Barrett (1808–76), who wrote on the 'Pastoral Office' in 1839 and more generally on ecclesiology in 1854.[10] In the next generation, after the internal conflicts within Methodism had somewhat subsided, came works of mature reflection from James Rigg (1821–1909) and Benjamin Gregory (1820–1900), who represent the apogee of classical Wesleyan ecclesiology. Rigg, who after 23 years in circuit was Principal of Westminster College for the rest of his active ministry, was the author of many occasional books and tracts, defending and expounding the Wesleyan position vis-à-vis other traditions. Gregory was more of a systematic theologian and, as such, was wider ranging in his ecclesiology. He was Connexional Editor from 1868 to 1893.[11]

Finally, in 1885 and 1891, come the works, respectively, of W. F. Slater (*Methodism in the Light of the Early Church*) and W. A. Quick (*Methodism, a Parallel*).[12] By that stage, however, a very different era of Methodist history and, indeed, ecclesiological thinking was beginning.

Standing rather apart from all these thinkers come Richard Watson (1782–1833) and W. B. Pope (1822–1903),[13] the great Wesleyan systematic theologians. Like the others cited, they belonged very much to the old Wesleyan tradition, but their account of ecclesiology is far more generalized and much less contextual than is the case with the others. For a brief note on their ecclesiology and the more generalized points made by Gregory, see below pp. 35–40.

Between them, the classic Wesleyans built up an impressive ecclesiological structure. They anticipated much that is said today ecumenically about the Church as *koinonia* or communion, about the exercise of episkope and about the relationship of ordained ministry and people in the Church. Their achievement has been too easily forgotten. In part, this is because of the mismatch between the ideal they advocated and the reality of the tensions and conflicts within the system they served. In part, it is also owing to the breakdown of the relative isolation of Wesleyan Methodism towards the end of the nineteenth century and the attenuation of its distinctiveness under a mixture of more generalized 'free churchiness' and Liberal Protestant theology. Perhaps another factor is their relative ecclesiological modesty. This may seem an odd statement in view of the triumphalistic claims of Rigg and others who asserted that Methodism had developed the most successful ever structures for mission and Christian nurture. However, even Rigg was primarily concerned with defending the legitimacy of Methodist ecclesiology rather than arguing that it necessarily held lessons for others. The Wesleyans were ambiguous about connexionalism, tending to see it more as a Wesleyan 'particular institution' rather than as a principle for the Universal Church, though we do find W. F. Slater arguing, at the very end of this period, that connexionalism might be a Methodist gift to the wider church.[14] His suggestion was, however, to remain dormant until Brian Beck and others began, over a century later, to raise the matter in debate.[15]

The Wesleyans presented a well-argued case for their ecclesiology which carefully integrated their understanding of the faith and Christian fellowship with their understanding of connexionalism and the role of the ministry. They combined a regard for scriptural principle, as they understood it, with a careful avoidance of any 'restorationism', that is to say any concept that the exact pattern of the Primitive Church either could be or should be exactly reproduced.[16] They continued the principled pragmatism of Wesley. They believed, as he had, that God had raised up Methodism and that her unpremeditated institutions had acquired legitimacy from their success in promoting both evangelism and nurture.[17] They also believed that the structural pattern of Methodism could be seen as consistent with the apostolic pattern of developing and adapting ministries and institutions as witnessed in the New Testament. The Wesleyans never tried to claim that any Methodist institution actually replicated the exact pattern of the apostolic Church. In any case, they realized, again well in advance of modern scholarship, that the

New Testament did not witness to any single pattern of church life or ministry as absolutely normative for all time. What they did claim is that Wesleyan patterns of ministry, connexion and fellowship were faithful to the basic patterns of the New Testament.[18] Thus, for example, Gregory ended his great work with a survey of the provision made at various stages of Christian history for close mutual fellowship. His aim was not to prove that the class meeting corresponded exactly with anything recorded in the New Testament but to assert that it made provision for a need recurrently felt throughout Christian history and that it provided for the mutual support and exhortation repeatedly recommended by Paul in his epistles.[19] The Wesleyans also made some appeal to a form of 'natural theology' in their ecclesiology. Thus, Barrett argued that, as well as building up the wider Church as a whole, connexionalism provided for that natural interdependence in human activities that was expressed, in secular and academic terms, by the existence of societies and universities.[20]

The Wesleyans also related their ecclesiology to their Arminian theology, their 'evangelical experimentalism', as Rigg and others called it. This necessitated, so they averred, both the oversight of a corporate ministry and the existence of cells of fellowship at the most local level. Rigg, indeed, believed that Methodism could not continue to exist authentically without them.[21] However, the Wesleyans never denied that other authentic churches could exist without such institutions. They were too much heirs to Wesley and the sermon 'On the Catholic Spirit' to do that. They were anxious, in total contradistinction to the Tractarians, never to 'unchurch' others, however critical they might become of them in the heat of controversy. The spirit of the famous 'Liverpool Minutes' of 1820 seems to have been retained.[22]

Relevant also to this discussion is the Wesleyan sense that their ecclesial development had been providentially guided to the specific situational requirements of the Revival. William James Shrewsbury contrasted the providential development of Methodist polity with the programmatic development of polity carried out by the Presbyterian reformers. The latter had created new structures from blueprints that they discerned in the New Testament. Methodism, by contrast, had evolved in an unpremeditated way. The Wesleys had not worked from presuppositions; rather, they had responded to the logic of the development of their movement.[23] James Rigg noted the similarity between New Testament developments and those of the Methodist revival. He commented: 'Of this the Wesleyans were not distinctly conscious at first. But, presently, they recognised the remarkable reproduction in their own society of the primitive and apostolic fellowship, and admired the more the manner in which they had been led by Providence.'[24]

For the Wesleyans, the structures that they developed were justified by their pragmatic effectiveness in evangelism and nurture. They believed that the New Testament laid down no prescriptive form of church order. Both the variety of church arrangements therein attested and the lack of specific injunctions concerning order were believed to support this claim. They also held that the New Testament witnessed to the pragmatic evolution of new ministries as required, the evolution of the diaconate in Acts 6 being the prime example of this.[25] James Dixon, writing almost contemporaneously with Shrewsbury, encapsulates this approach. For him, the divine purpose of the Church was certainly prescribed in Scripture as was the principle of the pastoral office. However, he continued:

Here we stop. The exercise of the Church's own liberty, or, rather, prudence and judgement starts at this point. What God has appointed can be subject to no modification by man. But the mode in which his truth is proclaimed and the discipline of his kingdom carried into effect, are not so limited and defined. Some scope for the exercise of judicious expediency is allowed. This is a mark of the wisdom of God. How can the same external forms be made to suit every time and place? . . . Ecclesiastical arrangements are not to be judged by their own independent character, but in accordance with the doctrines, spirit and designs of the Gospel.[26]

The title of Shrewsbury's fourth chapter of his *An Essay on the Scriptural Character of the Wesleyan Methodist Economy* eloquently illustrates the providentialist view. It is 'The Test of Scripture applied to Methodism, in a brief review of its rise, Progress and establishment, chiefly as illustrative of the Providential Government of God'. Shrewsbury argued that the Church 'was chosen for the theatre in which to display the manifold wisdom of God' and that this wisdom had been clearly shown in the evolution and success of Methodism, the 'distinguishing peculiarity' of which was 'an economy without invention ... gradually developed in a manner so entirely beyond human foresight or control, that it is evident that providential arrangement directed and consummated the whole'.[27]

'General' Ecclesiology

Watson and Pope were concerned to give an account of ecclesiology within the context of a general systematic theology. Though Watson intended his systematics as an Arminian counterblast to the contemporary Calvinist domination of evangelical systematic theology, he was influenced by classical reformed thought in his presentation of ecclesiology, emphasizing the Church particularly as a teaching and disciplinary institution. Apart from defending the Wesleyan view that no one system of church order or ministry could be regarded as definitive for all time, he did not really touch on specifically Wesleyan concerns.[28]

Pope was also concerned to enunciate his ecclesiology within the context of his overall systematic theology. He does not deal with specifically Methodist questions: there is, for example, no discussion of 'connexionalism' within his work, but his ecclesiology, like that of his near contemporary, Gregory, has an altogether Wesleyan 'feel' to it. Like Gregory's, it is highly pneumatological and doxological. He is, however, more ambivalent than Gregory on the question of Christian unity. He talked of the way in which the Church had 'lodged part of its authority' with the ministry, thus diluting the traditional Wesleyan emphasis upon the exclusive authority of the ministry.[29]

Gregory begins the *Holy Catholic Church* by citing Paul's great doxological vision of the praise of the Church continuing throughout all ages.[30] Pope's favourite biblical metaphor for the Church is that of 'temple'. Both emphasize the role of Christ and the Spirit. Pope says: 'The Church is the temple of Christ. It is inhabited by him. It is His body: the complement or fullness of Himself.' Gregory complements and goes further with this insight:

> The Church, in becoming the receptacle of Christ, becomes the fullness of Christ; after the same manner that His strength is made perfect in weakness ... the Church is to Christ the realisation and embodiment of His own full idea of spiritual beauty and perfection. The Church is His fullness of restful, blissful, consummate satisfaction, in loving and being loved again ... Christ's Headship of the Church is ... no mere honorary headship ... it includes the actual communication from Christ to His members of strength, peace, blessedness and purity, in fact of his own 'nature', and a reciprocal consciousness between Him and them.[31]

Gregory's doctrine of the Church is thus an extremely high one, going well beyond the purely functional. It has much in common with the vision of the twentieth-century Orthodox theologian, John Zizioulas, who has emphasized the corporate, inclusive nature of Christ.[32] It constitutes the deepest reception within the mature Wesleyan tradition of the mystery of corporate life in Christ as presented within the Pauline epistles. The key characteristic of the Church is its participation in the divine life, from which its functions of teaching and discipline then flow as important, but clearly subsidiary to the pulsating of the divine life within it. Gregory understands these functions in this way.

> The Church is to be the continuator on earth of Christ's work of invitation, teaching, restoration, sympathy and consolation, but not of atonement. With that express excep-

tion, it is the conscious and subservient instrument in carrying out the work which Christ initiated. It is the organ of
his highest action upon the world, and that not only by
authorization, but still more *derivation of life from Him* [my
italics] and by the fact that His Spirit is the animating
principle.[33]

Both Pope and Gregory also strongly emphasize the role of the
Spirit. For Pope, he is the 'source of all energy and strength to
the body of Christ upon earth'.[34] For Gregory, the Spirit is both
life-giver to the Church and giver of unity, the latter depending
on the continued presence of the Spirit within the Church, for
lack of which unity can only be the false unity of coercion. It
is, above all, the Spirit which prompts the Church to new acts
alike of mission and of recognition. Thus, in discussing
the admission of the Gentiles in Acts 11, Gregory cites Peter,
'What was I, that I could withstand God?'[35] It is the Spirit
that enables difficult decisions to be made freely and without
coercion. Commenting on the Apostolic Council in Acts 15,
Gregory writes: 'There was no crushing or cramping centralis-
ation ... no congestion. On the contrary, there was the freest
circulation of love throughout every part of the system.'[36]
Gregory's dictum points to a truly balanced understanding of
the Church as communion.

Gregory's belief in the constantly surging, and even innovat-
ing, life of the Spirit in the Church determined his attitude to
'development' and provides an interesting contrast with Pope's
perspective. For Pope, the day of Pentecost was paradigmatic
for the Church. Commenting on it, he says:

The elements of order, prepared in the Gospels, now take
their instant and permanent form. Pentecost is the typical day
of the future of Christendom; in the morning, the worshipping
assembly, glorifying God for the accomplishment of all his
purposes; in the noon, the full evangelical preaching; the rest
of it is given to organisation and fellowship.

Pope emphasized three elements. 'It is the CHURCH as gathered from the world; it is the CONGREGATION as gathered together; it is the FELLOWSHIP as replenished with common gifts. And these three ought to be one.'[37]

For Gregory, however, the emphasis was on the constantly developing life of the Church. Gregory was anxious that the understanding and definition of the Church should never be encapsulated within a formula that would inhibit further progress and development. He talked of an ideal that would be increasingly realized.

> Although no strict definition of the Church is given in Holy Writ, yet a clear and complete ideal is set forth; and that organisation is best which tends most strongly and securely to the realisation of that ideal. The ideal of the Church was not fully realised in Apostolic times, but is to be realised before the completion of the Church's history. All the church arrangements made by the Holy Spirit through the apostles are made with direct reference to the ultimate attainment of this perfection.[38]

Elsewhere, Gregory states that the Church, like the child Christ, had to grow in wisdom and stature.[39] He was no primitive restorationist but rather believed that 'the Primitive Church did not pretend to perfection, or to finality of external arrangement, or to be the Model Church'. Rather it was called constantly to press on to realize increasingly fully its ideal, tugged by its promised eschatological destiny, encapsulated in the Pauline phrase 'till we all come to the stature of the mature manhood of Christ'.

> That blessed destiny is not so much looked upon as future and final, as ever present in the mind of Christ . . . and therefore never to be absent from the mind of the Church as the great goal towards which we must heartily and hopefully strain.[40]

Linked to Gregory's understanding of the work of the Spirit in the Church and its constant potential for development is his apparently paradoxical attitude to its structures. He begins by stating a pair of paradoxes; first, that the Church is not 'a thing of rigid definition' and, second, that it is a definite community with 'a distinct object and reason of existence, a corporate and confidential fellowship upon plain, precise, peremptory conditions'.[41] He argues that the Church must 'body forth its hidden life in institutions', yet also, in general agreement with Wesleyan overall apologetic, he argues that nowhere are these exactly prescribed in the New Testament and certainly not for all time. He argues that much was left to the discretion of the apostles and that the contemporary Church, so far from being unable to alter what it has received, is even under the necessity of so doing if the exigencies of its mission compel it. He is sure that the Spirit guides the Church in such circumstances. 'The early churches acted less from prescriptions than from principles, and less from articulated principles than from intuitions.'[42] He is suspicious of any narrowing rigidity that may undermine the dynamic catholicity of the Church. Thus we find him saying: 'If we find that the Church is an institution, and not a mere ideal, that there is a real historical continuity . . . let us not cry, That is Popery . . . if we find an eager inclusiveness . . . let us not cry, that is latitudinarianism.'

His principle works to defend churches that have a real spiritual rationale for their principles.[43] Thus, he says of the Society of Friends and their rejection of order:

> The error of the Society of Friends, in the matter of church organisation, is that they presume to restrict the freedom of the Spirit, inasmuch as they will not allow Him to organise if He please, but will insist on His always acting in an incalculable and inconsequent manner.[44]

This last statement of Gregory's is perhaps relevant to Methodists as they discuss with Anglicans how the reception of the sign of the historic episcopate might better enable Methodism to express connexionalism across time.

Gregory is by far the most subtle and original of the Wesleyan ecclesiologists of this period, his thought ranging far and wide, not always totally systematically, but always fruitfully in terms of throwing out new ecclesiological theologoumena. Much remains for us to explore further within the context of more narrowly defined Methodist emphases and concerns.

We now proceed to examine various specific elements in 'classical' Wesleyan ecclesiology, looking at the doctrine of the ministry, including its relationship to the whole people of God, connexionalism, the understanding of fellowship in the class meeting, the understanding of relationships with other churches and Christian unity.

The Wesleyan understanding of the 'Pastoral Office' has been the most controversial aspect of Wesleyan ecclesiology, hotly contested by Independents and non-Wesleyan Methodists alike. Some scholars have tried to argue that it was effectively an invention of a key section of the Wesleyan hierarchy in the late 1820s.[45] It is true that there was little specific apologia for it at earlier dates, but it seems clear that Wesley, however much his views may have changed on the necessity of episcopal order as such, retained a strong doctrine of the ministry which he believed to be necessitated both by Scripture and by practicality. Few things distressed Wesley more than seeing a ministry not carrying out its God-directed functions. 'Who', he said, 'shall watch over them in faith and love?' Moreover, as the Wesleyan apologists repeatedly stressed, Wesley's practice seemed to imply a unique degree of authority for ministers, clearly distinct from that vouchsafed to lay leaders, such as local preachers, stewards or class leaders.[46] Such authority related both to their total separation from ordinary life and to their appointment by himself as one who, as an existing presbyter, came to believe he had such authority, and also as one clearly providentially raised up by God. In 1796, Joseph Benson clearly held the germ of what is sometimes alleged to be the later Wesleyan doctrine:

Ministers are not the servants of the people. Christ has entrusted the Church . . . not to the people but to the ministers of the Gospel . . . they are not at liberty to give up the steering or government into other or less skilful hands.[47]

The compromises of 1795 and 1797 are also relevant here. Though the local society 'leaders' meetings' were given a degree of coordinate authority at this time, final authority over the Connexion, as exercised through the Conference, was still reserved to the travelling preachers.[48]

The Wesleyans from Beacham and Bunting through to Rigg were fond of citing Hebrews 13.17 on obedience to pastors and arguing that pastors must have a degree of independence of lay interference if they were to discharge their duty accountably to God.[49] Rigg was as critical as any Tractarian of the way in which 'independent' pastors could be hired and dismissed by their congregations.[50] Barrett denied that there was any instance in Scripture of a minister being appointed by a congregation. Rather, he and other Wesleyans argued that ministers were always appointed by other ministers. In the apostolic age, this had been by the apostles themselves with the concurrence of the elders or other pastors. Starting from the Great Commission in Matthew 28.19–20, he argued that Christ's commission had clearly envisaged the need for continuing delegation of ministerial authority, and on this the apostles had duly acted.[51] A particular Wesleyan stress was on the corporate nature of this delegation. The Wesleyans argued that apostolic precedent normally implied a collective act of ordination; thus, Timothy had received the 'laying on of hands' of the presbytery as well as Paul. Waddy argued that Wesleyan Methodism was the only church in which 'the true Scriptural principle of the appointment of ministers was recognised and acted upon'.[52] Continuing corporate episkope was seen as important, not just for the 'connexion' as a whole, but for the body of ministers themselves, who exercised oversight over each other. Wesleyans regarded their ministry, not without reason, as the most effectively supervised in Christendom. The whole body of ministers was responsible for the selection of candidates for the ministry and for overseeing their probation, receiving them into full connexion, ordaining them and then continuing to watch over them to the end.[53]

Rex Kissack recognized that the Wesleyan doctrine of the ministry, as expounded by Alfred Barrett in his classical statement, *An Essay on The Pastoral Office* of 1839, was closer to that of the Tractarians than to that of the other nonconformists of the time.[54] It has, however, to be distinguished from the former in several ways. First, though continuity was emphasized, it was qualified in two ways. It had to be a continuity of 'faithful men'. Unfaithfulness, as Shrewsbury also stressed, would break the chain, since Paul had commanded Timothy to commit office only to 'faithful men'.[55] In such situations, God might raise up a new ministry without the usual authorization. Shrewsbury granted this as a theoretical possibility, though he preferred to rest the authority of the Wesleyan ministry on the line of authorization from Wesley as an existing presbyter.[56] He also stressed the fact that Wesley, from the beginning, had also sought in ministerial appointment and recognition the concurrence of those whom he had appointed as pastors.[57] Second, the Wesleyans, following Wesley's own conviction from 1746 onwards, believed that there was fundamentally only one order of ministry since the terms 'bishop and 'presbyter' had originally been interchangeable.[58] However, Barrett also emphasized that there was nothing wrong in ascribing presidency to particular ministers, to the annually elected President of the Conference, as temporary 'bishop of the whole Church', and to superintendents in their circuits. He believed that the 'angels' of the churches in Revelation had been such presiding ministers.[59] Barrett furthermore maintained that primitive bishops had been of this pattern, citing Cyprian's statement that he had never acted save in consultation with the presbytery.[60]

Barrett summarized New Testament nomenclature and functions of the ministry as follows,

Pastor or Teacher, Elder and Bishops, being the three approved distinctions in common of Christian ministers, we see everywhere that they are being used interchangeably, and

involve each other; that they refer to one order of men, pos-
sessing the same general rights, and charged with the same
general responsibilities ... As Pastors, they have to do with
a flock, as Elders they are denoted to have sufficiency of
wisdom and age; as Bishops they are obligated to examine
and inspect; as stewards they take care of the Lord's household and preserve his truth in the Lord.[61]

The Wesleyans emphasized strongly the fact that ministers were
set aside exclusively for their work. This they saw as essential
and also marking them off from other teachers or preachers such
as class leaders and local preachers; as Barrett put it, occasional
preaching does not impart the ministerial character.[62] Their itinerancy also marked them out. The Wesleyans did not, however,
try to argue that itinerancy was a necessary feature of the ministerial office, though they held that it brought many advantages.
They also felt that it reflected the practice of the apostles.[63]

Though the Wesleyans rejected the doctrine of the 'apostolic
succession' as understood by high Anglicans, they nevertheless
regarded their ministry as truly apostolic, making a careful distinction between those functions that they regarded as pertaining
solely to the original apostles and those that they believed continued to be handed down. Benjamin Gregory referred to the
travelling prophets of the sub-apostolic age, the 'apostoloi', as
forerunners of the itinerant Methodist ministers.[64]

Gregory also developed an understanding of ministers as
kingpins in the wider *koinonia* of the Church, facilitating unity
with the wider Church. He referred to the minister as the 'ruling
servant and serving ruler ... the impersonation of order and
harmony, the key-stone of the arch of unity'.[65] To put it in terms
of modern ecumenical ecclesiology, the ordained minister is the
one who exercises the ministry of *koinonia*, keeping the people
of his local church or churches in fruitful communion with each
other and with the wider Church. The fact that the minister
derived his authority from a body representative of the wider
Church rather than the local church acted as a permanent
reminder to the people of the nature of the Church Universal.

Gregory's assertion that the minister is the 'serving ruler' and
'ruling servant' brings us to the question of the relationship
between pastor and people, and especially the lay officials within
Methodism. All the Wesleyans emphasized the importance of
the lay officers of the Church. Rigg, in particular, maintained
that Methodism made far greater active use of its laity than did
any other church, including those that so prided themselves on
their lay government.[66] Nevertheless, he insisted as strongly as
anyone on the maintenance of the due, final authority of the
ministry. Rigg compared the appointment of stewards to that
of the diaconate by the apostles within the primitive Church;
clearly, he saw it as the duty of ministry to create and recognize
such auxiliary ministries.[67]

He also saw such lay officials as having very real rights which
he argued had not merely been safeguarded, but, within his own
lifetime, had been increased by the Conference.[68] Barrett linked
the very authority of the ministry in part to the protection of
these rights: 'The mass of the people composing the churches
have their rights; and Pastors, so far from infringing on these
rights, are placed in the Church especially to maintain them.'
Barrett stressed the importance of what he called the 'co-
working of people and pastors'. He argued that this had been
the pattern of the early Church. He instanced Cyprian readmit-
ting one of the lapsed, commenting 'not that they (the people)
had co-ordinate jurisdiction, but that this honour was due to
the faith and reverence of those who had stood firm in persecution'. He then added, to balance the starkness of ministerial
authority in the previous sentence, 'the importance of never
acting without the people' and adding 'bishops and presbyters
. . . only strengthened themselves by seeking for lay concurrence
and co-working'. He also added that it was the cessation of this
practice that had led to the later triumph of sacerdotalism and
distortion of the faith.[69] Shrewsbury, like Barrett, emphasized
the importance of co-working as a permanent principle. He
acknowledged that it was 'never the design of God to confine
employment in his service to the ministers of the Gospel'.[70] He
saw the outpouring of the Spirit at Pentecost as indicating and

enabling the participation of all the faithful, according to their gifts, in the work of mission. From the day of Pentecost onwards, 'there has never been a revival of real spiritual Christianity without the multiplication of agents to co-operate with God's servants in extending it'. Ministers and lay workers were essentially complementary. 'For just as the Church could not exist for any length of time without ministers, so neither with ministers could she flourish and prosper without suitable agents to assist them in stirring up the zeal of the members.'[71]

Both Shrewsbury and Barrett believed that there was a proper harmony between ministers and people. Shrewsbury asked how ministers could find a guarantee against lay despotism and how people could be ensured against the misuse of ministerial power.

The answer is that anxiety about this matter on either side betrays a want of grace in the heart and a distrust of the efficacy of the Gospel in the minds of men. The worst evil that can affect any Church is mutual suspicion between Ministers and People; and the greatest good to be desired and promoted is a generous and unlimited mutual confidence, disposing to habitual co-operation.[72] Barrett added, in similar vein:

There is indeed, a happy conjunction of influence among ministers and people, where all alike abide in the truth which answers the all-harmonising purposes of a political constitution, even while it aims at purposes far higher; but this is not brought about by what statesmen call 'balance of power', but by mutual fulfilment of a system of duty which Infinite Wisdom has arranged.[73]

It was left to Gregory to short circuit these rather convoluted statements by asserting clearly that the harmony and balance of the Church were clearly the work of the Holy Spirit and strictly dependent upon him for their continuation.[74]

Rigg, from 1850 onwards, sought to stand on essential Wesleyan principles while offering concessions that would give lay people more of a sense of involvement in the running of the Church, concessions that he argued were in any case justified by the growing education of the laity.[75] He always, however, maintained that demands for greater lay authority based on democracy were based on an essential confusion between what was appropriate in civil society and what was, according to Scripture and divine will, appropriate for the Church. He also argued that since the Church was essentially an aggressive force against disbelief and sin, its leaders, like those in an army, must have clear and final authority.[76]

The Wesleyan ideal was a high one, but in practice it was vitiated both by the arrogance of some in the ministry and by their 'bending' of the rules on certain occasions in order to combat what they saw as insubordination within the ranks of lay leaders.[77] Despite the theoretical affirmation of the 'lay' ministries of Methodism, insufficient tact was exercised by many ministers in practice. It was one thing for Rigg to affirm the vital contribution of local preachers as he did when he asserted that lay preaching was, above all, the key sign of the spiritual vitality of Methodism.[78] In practice, many local preachers did not feel valued as partners in the work.[79]

The holders of the pastoral office, ordained as the Wesleyan ordination service said as 'a godly example to the faithful', should perhaps have set a more positive example in the mutual trust for which Shrewsbury called. No doubt some lay officials were far from being the martyr heroes that later non-Wesleyan mythology made them out to be. Some, no doubt, were totally lacking in a sense of humility and respect for the unity and order of the Church, but some ministers had also forgotten that they were, as Gregory called them, '*serving* rulers'. Nevertheless, as the Latin tag has it 'abusus non tollit usum', abuse does not necessarily invalidate a practice. The Wesleyan understanding of due ministerial authority was not without its justification and is close to much in the modern ecumenical consensus. Bunting, for all his undoubted faults, was aware of the need to relate to the practice of the rest of Christendom when he advocated the restoration of the 'laying on of hands' in ordination.[80]

A final point to note was the Wesleyan emphasis upon the voluntary nature of the Connexion as morally and religiously necessitating acceptance of its discipline. Wesleyans neither denied the churchly status of other communions nor the right of people to choose to leave them in order to join another communion. While they believed that their emphasis upon the 'Pastoral Office' was scriptural, they did not deny that churches with a different discipline and a very different understanding of the role of the ministry had a right to exist as such. Since alternatives were available, it was unreasonable and unChristian for Wesleyans to seek to force changes in the discipline of a body that they had voluntarily joined and were free, at any time, to leave.

Connexionalism

Closely connected with the Wesleyan understanding of the pastoral office was the ecclesiological principle of connexionalism. It is important to emphasize right at the beginning that the Wesleyans did not claim that the connexional structures they knew and valued corresponded with any exact apostolic precedent. Rigg, in fact, accepted that the close connexionalism of contemporary Wesleyan Methodism would have been impossible within the system of communications then prevailing.[81] What he and other Wesleyans did claim was that connexionalism, as they knew it, encapsulated the spirit of the Apostolic Age and was markedly closer to its practice than were either systems based on independency or prelatical diocesan episcopacy as practised contemporaneously. They argued that the very practice of apostolic interference in the affairs of local churches showed that absolute independency was unknown to that age.[82] Some of their arguments were rather more forced and fanciful. Thus, we find both Barrett and Rigg endeavouring to argue, from the sheer size of the first church in Jerusalem, that it must have been a series of closely linked and associated congregations rather than a single church in the independent sense.[83] Rather more plausible is Gregory's argument based upon the action of the apostles towards the new churches, founded without their initiative by the Christians who fled from the first persecution in Jerusalem. Gregory recounted the visit of John and Peter to these churches, adding that they lost no time in *recognizing* and *connecting* them.[84]

Though the Wesleyans regarded the connexional system as both closer to biblical precedent and more effective in actual evangelistic effectiveness than rival systems, they never argued that it was of the 'esse' or essential nature of the Church. Perhaps, as has already been suggested, this was due both to an unwillingness to 'unchurch' others and to an awareness of the very distinctive innovations that dated only from the time of Wesley. However, it is clear that what was supremely important to them was the total sense of interconnectedness and interdependence involved. This no doubt owed something to the heritage of ecclesial awareness enshrined in Charles Wesley's hymns, which we have already discussed in chapter 1. It also owed much to the burning sense of mission. Wesleyans did not, following their founder, respect the concept of absolutely inviolably sacred parochial space, nor were they any more enamoured of the concept of 'gathered church' in the reformed tradition. They eschewed systems that seemed too narrowly ideologically bound. It is interesting, in this connection, to note Barrett's assertion that great harm had been done by those who had taken over-narrowly exclusive views of episcopal, presbyterian or independent polities.[85] British Methodist polity with its traditional emphasis upon just one order of ministry has sometimes been denominated as presbyterian, a position repudiated by Rigg, who argued that classical presbyterianism, as he knew it from the Church of Scotland, had neither the closeness of connexionalism nor the range of lay ministries, since the only persons sharing effective responsibility with the ordained ministry in the system were the 'ruling' elders.[86]

The classical Wesleyan case for the relative superiority of connexionalism as they knew it is well summed up by Rigg, invoking both overall scriptural principle and practical effectiveness.

Wesleyans find little difficulty in showing that their own system is in at least as close conformity with even the leading details of the primitive church arrangements as any other that may boast, however confidently, of its superior exclusive purity and scriptural authority. Still, it is not upon this fact that the Wesleyans ground their attachment to their peculiar institutions, so much as on the eminent adaptation of these to do the work of the primitive institutions in the present condition of the world, and to diffuse, unadulterated and unimpaired, the energy and influence of the apostolic gospel. And the peculiar excellence of the Wesleyan economy, in their view, is that it embodies more perfectly, and expresses more directly and fully, than any other, the genius, the spirit and tendencies, of primitive Christianity.[87]

Rigg's last sentence goes to the heart of the matter for the Wesleyans. Barrett argued that a connexional system was appropriate because of the needs of the *whole* of the Body. Local churches sometimes needed building up, and certainly supplying with pastors, from outside. Rigg pointed to the interlocking fellowship of local churches within a circuit as the essential context within which lay preachers could function. They could supply those places that could not every Sunday receive the ministrations of an ordained minister and they could open up and develop new work.[88] Shrewsbury saw connexionalism as the institutional expression of the Wesleyan virtue of 'disinterestedness', that is to say, a church system in which the missionary needs of the greater whole took precedence over the desires of any one local church and in which the ministers went where the Conference, rather than they as individuals, discerned the greatest need.[89] Rigg and Gregory both referred to the sense of mutual concern and aid that had suffused the apostolic Church and to the way in which the latter had been characterized by the finest possible 'circulation of love throughout the whole'.[90]

In his seminal articles on 'Connexionalism', Brian Beck argued that the Wesleyans had never really developed a theology of connexionalism.[91] In the sense of formal treatises, this is true, but the theology can be clearly teased out from their general works. There is no doubt that they believed that, in the apostolic

Church, there had been one mission and one sense of total interdependence prevailing throughout the churches. They accepted that this interdependence could not be given the degree of institutional embodiment that it was later, in an age of better communications, to be given by Methodism.

Though, in institutional terms, the Wesleyans were primarily concerned with 'connexionalism across space' rather than time, Gregory certainly manifested a strong sense of the Church's fellowship across time. He begins his great work, *The Holy Catholic Church* with what he describes as Paul's magnificent vision of the unending life of praise in the Church across the ages. He ends by citing Psalm 66.5, 'when they crossed the sea, then we did rejoice', as an indication of the solidarity in memory of the Church across the ages.[92] He also expressed some interesting opinions on the minutiae of apostolic church life which could not be received and developed in the context of his times. Thus, for example, he talked of the role of Peter in Acts 9.32, passing throughout all the churches in Palestine, as one who exercised 'itinerant superintendency' keeping them in connexion and exercising a real ministry of strengthening. It was not till the current stage of Roman Catholic–Methodist relationships that this insight could be fruitfully picked up and applied, as we shall see in the concluding chapter.[93]

Above all, the principle of connexionalism was linked to that of the corporate mutual oversight of the pastorate. From both followed the supreme authority of the Conference as the body through which all ministers and societies were linked and under whose authority both ministers and societies lay. The conjunction of the two principles explains the refusal of the Wesleyans to admit laymen to the Conference till 1878. Even then, it was still many years before lay people were allowed to be involved in the discussion of theological issues, the stationing of ministers or in election of the President.[94]

Inter-church Relationships and Unity

Officially, the Methodist line was one of friendliness to all other Protestant churches. The qualification 'Protestant' is to be noted. Classical nineteenth-century Wesleyans did not extend any proto-ecumenical olive branches to Rome. Even the ultra-irenic Shrewsbury denounced Roman error though perhaps less frequently than many of his Wesleyans contemporaries.[95] In this respect, the classical Wesleyan represented a decline from the rather ambivalent attitude of John Wesley who had combined a degree of anti-Roman polemic with more emollient approaches and observations, as when he said that he could tolerate superstition, even gross superstition among the Romanists on account of the genuine holiness of so many of their members.[96]

The official Wesleyan line was enshrined in a paragraph in the famous 'Liverpool Minutes', a series of Conference resolutions of 1820.

> Let us ourselves remember, and endeavour to impress on our people, that we, as a body, do not exist for the purposes of party; and that we are especially bound by the example of our Founder, by the original principle on which our societies were founded, and by our constant professions before the world, to avoid a narrow, bigoted and sectarian spirit, to abstain from needless and unprofitable disputes on minor subjects of theological controversy, and, as far as we innocently can, to 'please all men for good unto their edification'. Let us, therefore, maintain towards all denominations of Christians, who 'hold the Head', the kind and catholic spirit of primitive Methodism; and, according to the noble maxim of our fathers in the Gospel, be 'the friends of all and the enemies of none'.[97]

Clearly, this was a high ideal, scarcely likely to be honoured absolutely consistently at every level of the Connexion, but certainly one that influenced the classical Wesleyan ecclesiologists, particularly Shrewsbury and Gregory. The earlier classical

Wesleyans still retained a degree of affection for the Church of England. Shrewsbury defended the principle of establishment strongly.[98] Thomas Jackson argued that, as long as the Church of England remained Protestant, the Methodists would defend her.[99] By the time that Jackson gave this warning, the Oxford Movement was already beginning to have a considerable effect on the Church of England and Wesleyan affection for it was rapidly waning. Rigg commented in 1866 that Wesleyans no longer had the regard for the Church of England that had characterized their forebears.[100]

Nevertheless, the later classical Wesleyans, Rigg himself included, refused to join in the agitation of other non-conformists against the establishment. Rigg argued that though Methodists dissented from the discipline and dominant policy of the Church of England, they were not Dissenters on principle. They did not oppose in the abstract either 'establishment' or 'endowment'. 'They cannot see that it is a law of nature, or morals, or of the Gospel, that all church endowments are necessarily unlawful.'[101] Critical as Wesleyans frequently were of the older dissenters and especially of the Independents, they never denied their claim to be authentic churches. The Wesleyans continued to cherish their reputation for 'catholicity'. In this context they saw it essentially as involving the generous recognition of the work of the Spirit in other Christian communities, even those with which they had ecclesiological or other theological disagreements. Benjamin Gregory was particularly insistent that any community which was orthodox in its belief in the Trinity, in the two natures of Christ and in his atoning death, must be recognized as authentically a church.[102] The Unitarians were the only body he 'unchurched'. Even then, he accompanied his 'unchurching' with a generous tribute to the social rescue work carried out by Unitarians.[103] To Gregory, recognition of other Christian communities was an apostolic principle. As he said of the apostles themselves, 'whensoever, wheresoever and by whomsoever, the Spirit prompted church action, and gave the imprimatur of spiritual success, they at once recognised, reverenced and rejoiced in His work'.[104]

For Gregory, apostolic recognition was as important as apostolic succession was for his Tractarian contemporaries. Shrewsbury was particularly concerned that Methodists recognize that they were the 'debtors of all', of both Anglicanism and Puritanism in England and of elements in the continental Protestant tradition as well.[105] He was anxious that all churches cooperate in the great work of mission and recognize the particular gifts and contributions of each other.[106] He believed it was especially important for the Wesleyans to set an example in this matter. He stated that the aim of Methodism was never to proselytize but only to seek the spiritual welfare of all Christians and their denominations. He summed up the Methodist stance on what we would today call 'spiritual ecumenism' in these words.

It is the ordinary practice of men to pass by the excellencies of those whom they count opponents, and to fix only upon their defects or weaker points for the sake of gaining an advantage, a triumph, a victory; and this way of the world has too often been imitated in the churches of God, and even by ministers of the sanctuary. But the Wesleyans have not so learned Christ. It becomes them everywhere to 'rejoice in the truth', and wherever they meet with it in our common Protestant churches, to honour it and to observe its silent and gradual working with gladness of hearts; and it should be their joy to take every fit occasion of speaking of whatever will give the most favourable impression, consistently with truth, of every Christian community, and of all Christian ministers, without excepting those who, it is known beforehand, will only reward such generosity with envy and scorn.[107]

Shrewsbury coveted a role for Wesleyan Methodism as the 'middle link or bond of union' between the older dissenters and the Church of England.[108] He saw Methodism with its joint Anglican and Puritan heritage, exemplified in its dual heritage of liturgical and extempore prayer, as fitted for the role of 'middle link' or 'via media'.[109]

Shrewsbury defended the reasonableness of the established

status of the Church of England. He held that it was reasonable for a Christian ruler to use every means to promote the welfare, including the spiritual welfare, of his subjects.[110] He gave a more complex justification for the acceptance of 'establishment' by members of 'voluntary' churches. He based this on a subtle exegesis of the voluntary tribute offered by Araunah, the Jebusite king, to David (2 Sam. 24.20–4) and on the special advantages that establishment gave the Church of England in the pursuit of the common Christian mission. He saw the gracious acceptance of this by other churches as a real test of their 'disinterestedness' in the promotion of the common faith.[111]

> Let none then envy the dominant church, her superiority, or her privileges; and let not that church be arrogant or lordly in her carriage towards other churches; but let all combine in their several spheres, and in unison as often as they can, to promote 'glory to God in the highest, and on earth peace, goodwill towards men'.

He added that it was not unreasonable for one church, for historical reasons, to enjoy a generally recognized pre-eminence.[112]

Shrewsbury, Barrett (in his lesser writings) and Gregory all showed commitment to the ultimate unity of the Church.[113] However, in the circumstances of early and mid-Victorian Britain, this was scarcely a practical proposition. Occasional schemes were floated by Anglicans for some sort of reunion with the Wesleyans, but these were usually set in terms that Wesleyans could not possibly accept. Rigg's concept of unity was 'spiritual' rather than 'organic'. He believed that the separate denominations each had spheres of usefulness to which their social composition inclined them, and, as we shall see in the next chapter, it was partly on these grounds that he was sceptical even of reunion among the various branches of Methodism.[114]

In this context, however, the commitment of Shrewsbury, Barrett and Gregory is all the more remarkable and prophetic. Shrewsbury's commitment arose out of his extraordinary denominational humility and 'disinterestedness', to use his own expression, the tenor of which is reflected in the two verses of Charles Wesley that he cited in his book.[115] Barrett's vision was similarly based. He saw the failure of the Church to be united as a failure to grow *corporately* in grace. He argued that, all too often, people's hearts had been 'renewed' in conversion but not 'enlarged'. The remedy to this was the contemplation of God's manifold dealings with all the branches of his Universal Church and growth in mutual love which 'enlarges the heart'. Barrett further saw such enlarged vision as necessary to the full appreciation of all the riches of the gospel.

> A single Christian, yea, or a single Christian church, is a puny thing standing all alone, and does not see and feel and know *all* the Gospel, because the eye of the understanding and the heart of others is needed for this purpose. Christ intended the soul of his people to cohere, in order that, while they were mutually loving, they might mutually teach.[116]

Barrett continued with the reflection that the varying insights into the gospel, developed in separation, are in fact intended by God to be brought together into a deeper and richer common vision.[117]

It is, however, Gregory's understanding of unity which is richest, most profound and most clearly linked to the total Wesleyan theological vision. Gregory also anticipated much in the modern ecumenical ecclesiological consensus. Thus, he clearly roots the unity and *koinonia* of the Church in trinitarian theology.

'Christ Himself declared that the unity of the Godhead in the three persons of the Trinity is at once the archetype, basis and consummation of the unity of the Church.' He continues:

> as the life of the individual believer is to be manifested to the world, so it is designed that the unity of the Church should be manifested to the world. It is no part of Christ's plan that His body should be disjointed, that His Church should be split up into rival, mutually repellent or even isolated and altogether mutually independent fragments.[118]

Gregory also anticipated the modern emphasis upon the unity of the Church as inextricably linked to mission and to God's plan for the unity of humankind. In an important sermon delivered in his Presidential year, he defined unity as 'the grand object on which God has set his heart and mind'. Interestingly, he also defined it as 'an intuition of the human intellect ... a not yet wholly defaced feature of God's own image'. He argued that the life of the Church is characterized by a twofold search for unity, that of perfecting its own organic unity and the concomitant task of attracting the world into its unity. Both of these processes are attested in the Epistle to the Ephesians. Finally, he asserted that 'a united Church will soon include a united world. For, seeing this wonder the world will believe ... given a truly united, loving Church all nations will flow into it.'[119]

Gregory regarded the unity of the Church as essentially linked to its holiness. 'They only need despair of the unity of the Church who despair of its holiness.' He called the assumption that the perfection of the Church is merely an ideal a 'gross blunder'. The New Testament ideal of the Church is an ideal to be 'worked towards and ultimately attained', an ideal that will come about by 'kindly fraternal action and interaction of divers and universally diffused gifts of grace'. Paul's corporate promise of maturity in Ephesians points us to this; it is not 'till we each', but 'till **we all**' come. The 'divine ideal of the Church is a realisable ideal'.[120]

Gregory also threw out hints on ecumenical method. Unity can only come 'not by absorption, but by alliance and gradual sound assimilation, mutual attraction and approximation', in other words, by the process that ecumenists now call 'reception'.[121] He was convinced that growing cooperation in biblical study between the churches would materially aid the process. He was, unsurprisingly in view of his context, vague as to the exact shape of unity, at times talking of 'voluntary federation' which might seem a weak form of unity but for his insistence on assimilation and approximation.

It should, however, be noted that Gregory's contemporary, Rigg, did not think in terms of ultimate organic unity, even of the various branches of Methodism. After a discussion of the difficulties that would be encountered in reconciling the Wesleyan and non-Wesleyan polities, he added:

> How long is it since Methodists began to hold the view that organic unity is the true unity by means of which the kingdom of Christ is to be advanced? That has ever been the doctrine of the Roman communion and those churches that arrogate to themselves the title 'catholic' . . . but not the doctrine of the Protestant nonconformists.

Rigg also argued that each denomination occupied its own social 'niche', to evangelize which it was especially well fitted. Thus, he believed the evangelical style of the Primitive Methodists better suited to large sections of the working class than the Wesleyan. Mission did not require organic unity. Other Methodists agreed with Rigg, as, for example, the speaker at the 1891 Methodist Oecumenical Conference who regarded Christian unity as purely 'spiritual' and without implications for organic relationships, as such.

The Wesleyan Conference of 1890, replying to an invitation from the Archbishop of Canterbury to discuss the ecumenical potential of the 'Lambeth Quadrilateral' as approved by the Lambeth Conference of 1888 took a cautious line. It acknowledged that much more might be done to promote spiritual unity and cooperation. It deplored 'the schismatical spirit' but argued that the true unity of the Church did not require corporate union or the 'acceptance of any one form of polity and government'. It was sceptical about the 'historic episcopate' as a basis for reunion.[122]

Cumulatively, however, the contribution of individual classical Wesleyan theologians to ecumenical practice and theology was impressive, all the more so in an era of division when talk of such matters was not fashionable and when the views of people like Rigg were more widespread than the visionary attitude of a Gregory.

Fellowship and the Class Meeting

James Rigg defined the class meeting as the 'germ cell' of the whole Methodist system, 'the innermost institution . . . out of which the whole tissue and texture of Methodism has grown'.[123] He believed that Methodism without it would wither and die. It was the nursery of local preachers and the ministry, the place where the future members of both bodies first learnt to articulate their faith and do so in an acceptable and comprehensible manner; consequently, the demise of the class meeting would at least drastically reduce their supply. The class meeting was, moreover, essential to the evangelical experimental Arminianism that was at the heart of Methodism as the Wesleys and generations down to Rigg had understood it. In some sense, the class meeting was church in its most concentrated, intimate form. Rigg saw a necessary link between true evangelical experience and true evangelical doctrine.

> The Pentecostal inspiration can only be retained so long as not only the 'apostles' doctrine', but also the primitive fellowship is sacredly maintained . . . let the fellowship be dissolved and the doctrine even of experimental and evangelical theology will gradually become a mere sentimental theory of a latitudinarian type . . . When the primitive doctrine was rediscovered . . . the new converts instinctively gathered in bands.[124]

Gregory was just as emphatic in making that link. Discussing the meaning of the Greek word *proskaterountes*, translated as 'continuing steadfastly' in the Authorized Version, he comments:

> What is meant by 'giving themselves to the apostles' doctrine' is very plain. They devoted themselves to the learning, the experimental realisation and the assiduous practice of the truths which it was the principal work of the Apostles to teach.[125]

Both Rigg and Gregory were only too aware that, in one sense, the class meeting was very much a Methodist 'peculiar institution', one, in fact, of those 'prudential' means of grace that Wesley had identified. In contrast, they argued that it fulfilled a need that had always been felt by serious Christian believers but which had never formed, before the rise of Methodism, an integral part of church life for all within a particular tradition. Rigg argued:

> Methodist class meetings do but provide, in a regular way, for a universally felt spiritual necessity. Christians should hold free, intimate, yet guarded spiritual fellowship; they need to be instructed by each others' experience, to be mutually enlightened, encouraged comforted and admonished . . . Let clear, simple, effective provision be made for these things and we have the Methodist class meeting. Let the abortive and irregular attempts at mutual fellowship to be found in other churches be but made complete and something not materially distinguishable from the class meeting will be the result.[126]

To Rigg and Gregory, the class meeting was clearly of the 'bene esse' of the Church, extremely helpful, but not, as such, absolutely essential to being a true church. They reacted to suggestions from other quarters that Methodism was imposing an unreasonable test of membership in insisting on the discipline of regular meeting in class. Rigg countered, in part, by stressing that all churches tried to impose some test of seriousness before young people were admitted to full membership. Congregationalists and Baptists expected interviews with the deacons, prior to a recommendation from them and a vote at the church meeting. Anglicans insisted on confirmation which, at least in theory, was preceded by a catechetical test. Only Methodism imposed something that was expected to keep people permanently up to the mark.[127]

The later classical Wesleyans were concerned about the future of the class meeting. In the earlier half of the nineteenth century it had been taken for granted, but from the 1860s there were signs that its popularity was beginning to wane. As we have already seen, this filled Rigg with alarm for the future of Methodism. Many others shared his concern and only very gradually at the very end of the high Victorian period did the Conference begin to adjust its rules to take account of reality.[128]

John Simon, the leading expert on the Wesleyan Methodist constitution at the turn of the twentieth century, reminded Methodists of the disciplinary origins of the class meeting. He shrewdly noted that there was a tendency for 'fellowship', in a weaker sense, to overshadow the element of 'mutual oversight', though he showed equal concern that true fellowship, in terms of a common experience, should be maintained. For Simon, as for Rigg, the class meeting was central and its decay would imperil any justification for the continuation of Methodism as a distinct church.[129] S. W. Christophers stressed the original role of the classes in promoting holiness and seeing that all 'walked by the same rule'. Like Rigg, he feared that Methodism would decay if the class meeting fell into disuse.[130]

The Golden Mean

We may sum up the achievement, and boast, of Wesleyan ecclesiology, by saying that it claimed a particular and providential balance for the structures of Methodism. There was no intention of 'unchurching' other evangelical, Protestant churches; nevertheless, the Wesleyans believed that they had been providentially led to adopt ecclesial structures that were both closer in spirit to the ethos of the New Testament than those of the other main churches and more effective in terms of contemporary mission and nurture.[131] James Rigg, in particular, contrasted Wesleyan Methodism with the other main churches in both respects. He believed that Methodism had been providentially led to develop structures which, like those of the apostolic Church, allowed for the finest circulation of love, insight and fellowship and which were the best equipped to sustain effective evangelism and nurture. He agreed that these structures did not represent an exact replication of those of the apostolic Church. That was not necessary; what was necessary was that they subserved the same overall aims.[132] Rigg maintained that Methodism had rediscovered the vital link between doctrine and fellowship which allowed the flourishing of that 'evangelical Arminianism' that he regarded as alone authentic in contradistinction to a hard and speculative Calvinism or the superstitious 'sacerdotalism' of Rome and its Anglo-Catholic imitators. He asserted, 'The doctrine and the fellowship cannot long be maintained in vital reality apart from each other . . . the evangelical experience not only answers to the saving doctrine – it tests, preserves and reproduces it'.[133] Hence the importance of the class meeting just discussed.

Rigg believed that Methodism had preserved the right balance between the prerogatives of the ministry and the rights of the people. He believed that Methodism had not only preserved the correct understanding and practice of the pastoral office in contrast to independency and dissident Methodism, but had also provided adequate safeguards against its abuse and a role for the laity in church affairs that had expanded as Methodism had grown as the laity developed in experience.[134] Methodism had also given the laity a larger active role in the spiritual life of the Church than had the more 'democratic' congregationalist denominations. Both Rigg and Gregory saw this as a key point of Methodist superiority.[135] Shrewsbury also concurred in the view that Methodism used the laity more effectively than any church had since apostolic times.[136] Rigg particularly lauded the way in which Methodism had grown according to natural spiritual laws:

> Methodism is . . . in fact, the product, not of art, but of experience; it is not so much a mechanism as a growth, it is not the creation of theory . . . it is, from first to last, the outgrowth of living work, and has developed, at every step, in response to actual and well tested need.[137]

Methodism contrasted favourably with episcopalianism, presbyterianism and independency. Its superintendents, chairmen and presidents of Conference gave it some of the characteristics of episcopacy, but without the drawbacks of monarchical episcopacy or any danger of becoming purely a 'clergy church'.[138] It had much in common with presbyterianism, a point made earlier both by Watson and Bunting, but it was distinguished from Scots Prebyterianism by its greater role for the laity and the itinerant ministry.[139]

To Rigg and other classic Wesleyans the itinerancy of the ministry and its corporate episkope were particularly important. Rigg argued that the itinerancy of the ministry preserved it from becoming the captive of sectional local interests.[140] Shrewsbury also asserted that the discipline of itinerancy was a sign of the 'disinterestedness' of the ministry, the sole concern of which was the success of the overall mission rather than the satisfying of the predilections of individual ministers or local churches.[141] Rigg argued that the corporate mutual episkope of the pastors ensured doctrinal orthodoxy to a degree that contrasted particularly with both Anglicanism and independency where ministers could champion maverick views from the safety of a parson's freehold or personal hold over a local congregation.[142]

In short, the Wesleyans were convinced that their system, though necessarily imperfect and in need of periodic adjustment, was the best yet devised in Christendom. We may leave the last word with Rigg:

> The true mean as to government and discipline is to be found mid-way between the episcopalian theory and that of congregational independency . . . the true mean recognises the fact that Church movements, Church organisation, the very existence of a Church depend, in the first instance, on the action of the ministers of Christ, but nevertheless that, in the spirit of the primitive Church, provision must be made . . . for the creation of officers and helpers from amongst the members . . .[143]

The Ecclesiology of Non-Wesleyan Methodism

Reference has already been made to the degree to which the Wesleyans were stimulated ecclesiologically by their conflict with Methodist critics, both seceders from Wesleyan Methodism and members of independently formed connexions. Theirs was an alternative vision of Methodism that they tried to justify theologically. There were differences of emphasis as between the various non-Wesleyan traditions. The most conservative, and first to appear, was the Methodist New Connexion, founded in 1797. Its leaders later claimed, after the appearance of more radical Methodist churches, to follow a 'juste milieu' between the extremes of ministerial autocracy within the Wesleyan Church and the opposite extreme of lay domination that treated stipendiary ministers virtually as hired servants with little real status or authority.[144] In 1897, only 10 years before its union with the Free Methodists (United Methodist Free Churches) and the Bible Christians, W. J. Townsend and Thomas Rider continued to defend the polity of the New Connexion as maintaining a proper balance between the due prerogatives of the ministry and the rights of the people. Townsend argued that the New Connexion had been established 'not more to vindicate the proper standing of the laity in the Church than to obtain for the ministry its proper functions and prerogatives'. The New Connexion had established a 'ruling eldership', which closely resembled presbyterian practice. However, it had also balanced the power given both to 'ruling' and 'teaching' elders by a concurrent insistence upon the representation of elected layfolk at every level in the Church. Thus, it had incorporated the best elements of presbyterian and congregational practice in a way that was held to reflect the practice of the apostolic Church in which decisions had been made by the apostles and elders with the concurrence of the whole Church. Townsend concluded: 'the divine right of the ministry to rule and to teach was safeguarded in the Methodist New Connexion, but so also was the right of the people to be consulted and to have ultimate control of church arrangements'.[145] The New Connexion position was particularly positive. It did not seek to downgrade the ministry, but it did aim at emphasizing the corporate authority of the whole people of God.

It is also interesting to note that the New Connexion, also uniquely among the non-Wesleyan churches, produced general as well as defensive ecclesiology. The non-Wesleyan traditions, in general, confined themselves to apologias for their particular polities, cast in terms of denial of the rightness of Wesleyan or Anglican practice. Generalized statements might be made about the Church as mission or fellowship, but little was said about the wider position of the Church in God's plan. By contrast, Townsend and Rider had interesting ecclesiological theologoumena to adduce. Townsend discussed the relationship of Church to Kingdom and was as firm as Gregory upon the necessity of embodied rather than 'spiritual' unity. 'Whatever tends towards this end must have the special benediction of the Master upon it and grave is the sin of those who would cause or needlessly perpetuate divisions in the body of Christ.'[146] In true Wesleyan style, Rider added to the Lutheran concept of justification by faith as the 'article of faith by which the Church stood or fell', the concept of holiness as equally such a mark of the Church in pilgrimage. 'It is no less true that the doctrine of holiness is the mark of a progressing and victorious Church. This growth is a sign of the Church's pilgrimage towards that state that is "without spot or wrinkle".'[147]

A key emphasis in all the non-Wesleyan connexions was on the co-pastoral authority of class leaders. A major point in the apologetic of the Reformers of 1849–51 was that itinerant ministers, precisely because they changed station so frequently, could scarcely be considered regular pastors in the same way as class leaders.[148]

There was a fundamental clash between two interpretations of the origin and rise of Methodism. For the Wesleyans, the authority of Wesley and his preachers was paramount. God had providentially raised them up. They had originated the movement and consolidated it. The lay people of Methodism had voluntarily placed themselves under their guidance and were

bound to continue to accept it or to leave the movement peace-
fully. The preachers had conceded certain rights to the leaders'
meetings in 1795 and 1797 in the interests of harmony and
justice, but these concessions in no way negated their divinely
given pastoral authority. The non-Wesleyan Methodists interpreted the history differently. They saw Methodism as resting
upon a contract between the preachers and the people, in which
the preachers would not exceed their rights. No amount of
emphasis upon the 'pastoral office' could convince the non-
Wesleyans that ministers were pastors in a sense that class
leaders never could be. The other Methodists were convinced
that it was the inner circle of Wesleyan ministers that were the
destructive innovators in the period 1820–50, destroying the
true balance of Methodism and thereby obliging many to leave
it. To the Wesleyans, the reverse was true: the non-Wesleyans
were claiming a role for laypeople in the final courts of
Methodism that they had never had and should never have.[149]

Though there was some link between political radicalism and
the demand for greater lay participation in church government,
the reformers did not adopt the democracy of the 'church meeting' as known in the independent tradition. Rather, as has been
stressed by some historians, they championed a form of lay
official oligarchy in the churches, a point that did not escape
the notice of Wesleyan apologists who riposted that the people
had no more authority over the largely self-appointed lay oligar-
chies than they had over the ministry in the Wesleyan system.
Furthermore, according to the Wesleyans, whereas the pastoral
office had a clear scriptural basis for its prerogatives, the lay
oligarchy had none.[150]

One of the biggest differences in ecclesiology between Wesleyans and non-Wesleyans lay in the appeal of the latter to
analogies with the British Constitution. One dissident Wesleyan
layman of the early nineteenth century alleged that his 'civil
rights as a Briton and Scriptural rights as a Christian' were
violated in Wesleyan theory and practice.[151] The Wesleyans
always argued that the former considerations were irrelevant;
there was a clear distinction between authority in the state which

required consent and authority in the Church which was divinely confided to those who held the pastoral office. The non-Wesleyans repudiated any such idea.[152]

Another difference existed in respect of order. The 'imitative' movements, in particular, accused the Wesleyans of being too obsessed by order.[153] To a degree, they could appeal to Wesley's own precedent and to such remarks as 'Church or no church, I must attend to the saving of souls'. Both the founders of Primitive Methodism and of the Bible Christians had lost their status as Wesleyans because of irregular preaching.[154] They and their followers believed that, in persisting with their activity as they did, they were returning to the spontaneity of 'primitive' Methodism, hence the self-ascriptive name of the largest of all the non-Wesleyan churches.[155] In emphasizing one aspect of the Wesleyan heritage, they tended to ignore another, the emphasis upon disciplined growth and nurture in faith, the very emphasis that explained the nature and growth of the connected societies. They wanted ministers who were, at least at the beginning, hired evangelists. Bunting, however, claimed of the Wesleyan ministry, 'our proper office is to be pastors and teachers. I believe that we are teachers to instruct and pastors to govern the people.' So, far from wishing their ministers to undertake this task, the non-Wesleyan Methodists, in particular, made every effort to restrict them. The Wesleyan Methodist Association allowed local preachers to carry out any liturgical role, including sacramental ones. The Protestant Methodists put all power into the hands of 'elders', to be elected for annual terms by the Quarterly Meeting. They made the plan, provided for the administration of the sacraments and issued class tickets.[156]

Though all the non-Wesleyan Methodists claimed to wish to preserve connexionalism, they all diluted it in favour of increased authority for the local church and the circuit. They saw connexionalism as primarily a matter of the voluntary association of the like-minded rather than a system of mutual accountability, let alone a vital embodiment of the inner *koinonia* of the Church Universal. The Wesleyan Reform Union was quite explicit: 'while desirous of maintaining the connexional principle, we hold that all local church courts are independent and their decision is final'.[157] The United Methodist Free Churches emphasized the autonomy of circuits, though it did place two restrictions upon them; they could not subdivide themselves without authority of the Assembly, the nationally representative body, which also had the right to expel heretical circuits. It should also be noted that many United Methodist Free Churches circuits were single station and thus virtually congregationally independent.[158]

The Independent Methodists and the Wesleyan Reform Union in particular made it clear that they had a purely associational, congregational doctrine of the local church. The former defined themselves as follows: 'We are companies of believers in Jesus Christ. These churches have no authority but what the members confer. Each church is an entity of itself. The Annual Meeting [i.e. the annual representative meeting of Independents] is deliberative.' The Wesleyan Reform Union added 'A Christian church is a company of believers in the Lord Jesus Christ, Saviour of the World, who meet together for the worship of God, and for mutual counsel.'[159]

Effectively, these two churches had a purely congregationalist ecclesiology, albeit that they respected and lived by the Wesleyan understanding of the faith as such. This descent into pure congregationalism no doubt explains why these two churches found it impossible to enter into Methodist reunion in 1932, whereas the other churches found it eventually possible to compromise with the Wesleyans once the latter had conceded the principle that lay people could sit in the highest courts of the Church. We shall examine this, along with other issues, in the next chapter.

3

Ecclesiology from Hughes to Flew

This chapter deals with the main ecclesiological developments within Methodism from 1890 until about 1950. The influence of Hugh Price Hughes (1847–1902) is taken as the starting point.[1] Hughes was not a systematic theologian or ecclesiologist as such. Nevertheless, his influence on the future direction of Methodism was profound. More than any other single person in his generation, he was responsible for re-orientating the Wesleyan Connexion away from the conservative stance of Rigg and Gregory and creating a new ethos in which Methodism's understanding of its mission became much broader. At the end of the period Robert Newton Flew (1886–1962) was the dominant ecclesiologist, representing British Methodism frequently on the World Council of Churches and masterminding the first major ecclesiological report of reunited Methodism in 1937.[2]

Wesleyan Methodism emerged from its earlier relative isolation, in the process growing much closer to the other free churches and the rest of Methodism. At first, the mid-Victorian trajectory away from Anglicanism continued even though, from the very beginning of the period, Hughes hoped for and sought better relationships with the Church of England. From the 1920s relations with the Church of England began to improve, particularly at the level of church leadership.[3] This was true also of the leaderships of the two main non-Wesleyan churches, the United and Primitive Methodists. The famous Lambeth 'Appeal to All Christian People' had a striking effect on some free church leaders. The Primitive Methodist Conference in 1926 spoke of the 'nobility of the Lambeth Appeal itself' and of the way in which it had 'lifted the whole question of Reunion to a loftier level and into a new and sweeter atmosphere'. The United Methodist Conference went even further in endorsing the emerging ecumenical consensus that episcopal, presbyteral and congregational elements would all be equally essential within the constitution of a reunited Church. It is true that the Primitive Methodists also added that the 'time (for reunion) is, indeed, not yet ripe'. However, the changed attitude of some within both churches, until 1920 traditionally more suspicious of Anglicanism than the Wesleyans, was remarkable.[4]

Wesleyan Methodism was exposed to four new influences, all of which modified its life. First was the acceptance, after a relatively short struggle, of the principles of modern biblical criticism.[5] The second was a profound modification of its evangelical heritage through the influence of the popular Liberal Protestantism that had already begun to penetrate deeply into the other Methodist and free churches. The third was a strong 'social gospel' consciousness. Finally, came the influence of the Ecumenical Movement, though in the earlier part of the period this was largely confined to the leadership rather than the 'grass roots' of Methodism.[6] The first three of these changes came quite rapidly. Wesleyan Methodism was relatively late in its reception of modern biblical criticism. There were one or two sharp debates, as over Agar Beet's writing on eschatology, but within less than a generation the new criticism had become generally accepted. By 1914, the ethos of Methodism, in all its branches, was increasingly 'Liberal Protestant'.

These influences did not point in a uniform direction. The early stages of the Ecumenical Movement made Methodist leaders and theologians more aware of the strong points in the ecclesiology of others, whilst the growth of Liberal Protestantism and the movement towards Methodist reunion probably made many Methodists feel more consciously 'free church' in their ecclesiology. Certainly, one notes a down-playing of distinctively Wesleyan emphases. Little is said about 'connexionalism' in this era, though A. W. Harrison, writing in 1938, could still commend the concept of a 'connexional spirit' as counteracting 'denominationalism' and helping to create an

ethos favourable to ecumenism.[7] The understanding of the 'Pastoral Office' was considerably diluted, though it is clear that an
attenuated understanding of it remained important for some,
especially in the Wesleyan ministry.[8] Maldwyn Hughes, in his
Christian Foundations, enunciated an understanding of ministry
that reconciled aspects of the newer, more 'democratic' understanding of it with the traditional Wesleyan view. He emphasized, as had all Methodists of previous generations, the
importance of the 'inward call'. He also stressed approval and
testing by the Church. Finally, he argued that the minister 'dis-
charges a priestly office as a representative of the priesthood of
all believers' and approved by them; however, 'the authority is
not derived from them but from Him who called him to be
an ambassador, beseeching men on behalf of Christ'. He thus
preserved a delicate balance in the understanding of the 'representative' nature of the ministry that remains of value for
ecumenical dialogue and is arguably justified by a thorough-
going ecclesiology of *koinonia*.[9]

There can be no doubt that, for most Methodists at the grass
roots, the most important developments were those leading to
Methodist reunion. That is where we shall start. Subsequently,
we will look at the particular ecclesiological contributions of
Hughes, Lidgett, Joseph Agar Beet and A. S. Peake. Finally, we
shall examine Flew and Methodist involvement in early ecumenical ecclesiology.

Methodist Reunion

The first steps towards Methodist reunion had already been
taken before the beginning of this period. At first they were
confined to the smaller churches. The Wesleyan Methodist
Association, the Protestant Methodists and some of the
'reformers' of 1849–51 united as the United Methodist Free
Churches in 1857.[10] In 1866, the New Connexion approached
the Wesleyans for the first time with a view to the possibility of
reunion.

The initial attitude of most Wesleyan leaders was lukewarm.

Rigg, and many other Wesleyan conservatives, believed that the ecclesiologies involved, and particularly the understanding of the role of the ministry, were incompatible. Quite apart from this, Rigg believed that differing sections of Methodism (he especially instanced Wesleyans and Primitives) had distinctive missions to differing sections of society.[11]

When the matter was debated at Conference in 1887, the voting on resolutions showed a clear division between more conservative Wesleyans like Rigg and progressives like Hughes. For non-Wesleyans and for progressive Wesleyans, the matter was becoming increasingly practical politics. The admission of laymen to the Wesleyan Conference in 1878 meant that non-Wesleyans could now be assured that there was no longer quite the gulf over authority that there had been.[12] A New Connexion writer in 1897 could still emphasize that the Wesleyans had some way yet to travel; there were still, to his mind, too many matters exclusively reserved to the pastoral session of Conference.[13] However, further developments were encouraging from the non-Wesleyan point of view. Gradually, the scope of the Representative session of the Wesleyan Conference was enlarged. In 1908, for the first time, provision was made for ordinary Wesleyan church members to elect a certain number of representatives to the Leaders' Meeting. Wesleyan statements on membership, issued in 1908 and 1913, showed significant shifts towards the ethos of the non-Wesleyan churches. The definition of the Church began with the assertion that it was 'the company of His disciples, consisting of all who accept Him as son of God . . . and who join hands to work out their common salvation'. In language foreshadowing that of the Deed of Union (1932), it was stated that ministers 'have no exclusive title to the preaching of the Gospel or the cure of souls', thereby meeting the one-time grievance of so many who had split from Wesleyan Methodism in the first half of the previous century that the ministry of local preachers and class leaders had been under-valued vis-à-vis that of the ordained. Great emphasis was placed upon the brotherly fellowship of Methodism, a point also emphasized by the leading non-Wesleyans of this period who championed Methodist reunion. The importance of the class meeting was yet again reiterated, the emphasis being upon 'brotherly intercourse', 'mutual counsel' and 'building up in love'. Though meeting in class was no longer prescribed as absolutely essential, the Wesleyan people were reminded that 'the benefit received from it is greatly impaired by irregular attendance, and our people are earnestly enjoined to make constant use of this treasured means of grace'.[14]

In 1907, the United Methodist Free Churches, the Bible Christians and the New Connexion all united as the United Methodist Church.[15] In 1913, serious conversations between the three main branches of Methodism, Wesleyan, Primitive and United, began.[16]

The exigencies of mission and resources and the trauma and post-war idealism of World War I all contributed to the case for Methodist union. In many areas, particularly in Cornwall, which had been extensively worked over by all branches of Methodism, there were excessive numbers of small Methodist chapels, some of them almost next door to each other. Though, in the event, it proved very difficult to persuade many of these chapels to amalgamate, there was certainly a strong feeling that Methodism should unite and avoid duplication of resources.[17]

Contributing towards such sentiments was an increasingly strong sense of common Methodist identity, partly, though certainly not wholly, occasioned by reaction to the developing strength of Anglo-Catholicism in the established Church. The leading Wesleyan layman of the time, Sir Robert Perks, argued that it was time to forget the quarrels of their grandfathers' time. The New Connexion minister, W. J. Townsend, argued that differences between the various connexions were lessening and that, in particular, there was now a common sense of partnership between ministers and laity in church affairs that transcended the old divisions and quarrels.[18] George Eayrs's book of 1909, *British Methodism, As It Is, As It Was, As It Will Be: A Popular Handbook and History to Help Methodist Union*, gives an interesting indication of the drift of opinion at the time and the common ecclesiological basis upon which union was to be constructed. Eayrs testifies to the modification of attitudes on the part of Wesleyans and other Methodists alike. Of his own connexion, the United Methodist Free Churches, he says:

> In the UMFC, a sincere attempt was made to combine con-nexional rule with independency for the local church. Fifty years of history showed that connexionalism and Conference supremacy were of the essence of Methodism. They tri-umphed over the tendency to separatism.

He further argued that there were four characteristics common to the whole of Methodism. First, a sense of warmth and hearti-ness; the Church was a family. Secondly came a desire to involve everyone as fully as possible in the service of the Church to the world. Thirdly came liberality in giving and, finally, 'aptness for organisation and method'. He also made much of itinerancy and of the doctrine of the 'priesthood of all believers'. This last doctrine had, in fact, *pace* Eayrs, been as vigorously asserted by Wesleyans as by anyone. For the Wesleyans it had meant that no one could come between the soul of a Christian and his or her free access to the Father in the Spirit in prayer and inter-cession. The Wesleyans had not seen the doctrine as in any way incompatible with their understanding of the pastoral office and due church order. Eayrs, in common with many other non-Wesleyans, viewed the matter differently. He argued that the Wesleyans had, in former times *practically* denied the doctrine of the priesthood of all believers; now, however, they accepted the real partnership of ministers and laity.[19]

It was over continuing difficulties with the understanding of the ordained ministry that most of the problems came. About a third of the Wesleyan ministry felt that the scheme would undermine their doctrine and practice and tried to delay the union. They were concerned about the alleged doctrinal laxity of the other churches.[20] Contrariwise, there was some concern among the latter that the Wesleyans were too rigidly bound to the works of Wesley as doctrinal standards.[21]

The final scheme of union represented a compromise. The

Conference was to have a representative and a pastoral session following the Wesleyan practice, but the powers of the latter were to be much more limited than in the Wesleyan system. In order to meet atavistic non-Wesleyan fears of Conference as a centralizing and dictatorial body, circuits and districts were to be allowed to 'memorialize' Conference with their concerns. An innovation was the introduction of a lay Vice-President of the Conference. Originally a largely symbolic appointment, it underlined the principle of partnership between ministers and laity which everyone agreed should characterize reunited Methodism.[22]

Central to the ecclesiological understanding of the newly united church are the doctrinal clauses of the Deed of Union. They begin, in fact, with an ecclesiological statement.

The Methodist Church claims and cherishes its place in the Holy Catholic Church which is the body of Christ. It rejoices in the inheritance of the apostolic faith and loyally accepts the fundamental principles of the historic creeds and the Protestant Reformation. It ever remembers that in the providence of God Methodism was raised up to spread Scriptural Holiness through the land by the proclamation of the evangelical faith and declares its unfaltering resolve to be true to its Divinely appointed mission.[23]

This statement clearly echoed the current ecumenical context. Methodism asserted, both for the benefit of its ecumenical partners and in continuing refutation of Anglo-Catholic and Roman Catholic denial of its ecclesial authenticity, its claim to be a part of the one holy, catholic and apostolic Church. The term 'cherishes', when taken in conjunction with the ensuing statements, clearly implies Methodism's claim to embody an authentic 'typos' of Christian life. Such a claim in no way implies an adverse judgement upon any other church or churches that may profess the same authentic faith but with a different style of worship and mission and order.

The following statements about Methodist acceptance of the fundamental principles of the historic Creeds and the

Reformation contain a degree of ambiguity. The former is perhaps easier to interpret. A distinction is made between the exact wording of the Creeds and the truths they are meant to enshrine. The words, as such, cannot necessarily be accepted as final for all time; there may be alternative and better formulae to come as the Church grows in understanding. At the same time, however, there is a clear acknowledgement that behind the words, however inadequate and contextual, lies the unchanging truth of the apostolic tradition. The fundamental principles of the Protestant Reformation are more difficult to specify, since not all Protestants would agree upon them. Clearly, in view of the unanimously Arminian tradition of Methodism, they cannot be understood as embracing a doctrine of predestination. Presumably, they would include justification by faith, itself specified by Wesley as the 'strong rock and foundation of the Christian religion, that first drove Popery out of these kingdoms'[24] and the understanding that Scripture judges Tradition rather than vice versa. Finally, there is mention of the providential rise of Methodism and its central emphasis on Christian holiness. Noteworthy here is the emphasis upon doctrine rather than upon doctrine and discipline taken together. The Wesleyan emphasis upon 'watching over in faith and love' and 'minding all our discipline' had long since been attenuated.

The statements that follow on biblical and doctrinal authority represent a conflation of the traditional Wesleyan emphasis upon the authority of Scripture and, secondarily, of Wesley's writings. The divine revelation is said to be 'recorded' in the Holy Scriptures, not identical with them, a formula that owed much to the work of the Primitive Methodist scholar A. S. Peake and to Scott Lidgett. It reflected the position generally taken by twentieth-century Protestant biblical scholars. The desire of the Wesleyans to assert the continuing value of Wesley's standard works, and the reluctance of some non-Wesleyans to accept these, were met by the statement that the Notes and Sermons were 'not intended to impose a system of formal or speculative theology on Methodist Preachers' but rather to 'secure loyalty to those fundamental truths of the gospel of redemption' that all Methodists shared, presumably with other evangelical Christians.

Not surprisingly, the question of the ministry occupies about half of this document. Non-Wesleyan fears were in particular met in the statement that ministers had 'no exclusive title to the preaching of the gospel or the cure of souls'. The former had never been in doubt in Wesleyan Methodism, but classical Wesleyan theology, as we have already seen, had regarded the ministry and authority of class leaders as strictly dependent upon that of ministers. The ensuing statement, that 'these ministries are shared with them by others to whom also the Spirit divides His gifts severally as he wills' was clearly designed to underscore the belief that ministers had no exclusive cure of souls and that the ministries of class leader and local preacher were real ministries given and empowered by the Spirit.

Great emphasis was placed upon the 'priesthood of all believers' and the fact that ministers did not hold, nor did they acquire through their ordination, any 'priesthood differing in kind from that which is common to all the Lord's people'. Ministers were described as 'stewards in the household of God and shepherds of his flock'. These titles echoed those used in traditional Wesleyan apologetic, but there was no attempt to reassert it. Their role in 'directing' was mentioned and the need of special skills. In this context the phrase 'the principle of representative selection' was used upon which much of the later Methodist doctrine of presbyteral ministry was subsequently to be built.[25] The two sacraments of Baptism and the Lord's Supper were recognized as being of 'divine appointment and perpetual obligation'. In an age when many Liberal Protestants were inclined to question the value and necessity of the sacramental principle, this was an important statement.[26]

The ecclesiology of the Deed of Union is thus the ecclesiology of a church conscious of its heritage but also conscious of the need to harmonize sub-traditions between which some differences of emphasis remained. It sought to give an account of the sources of authority in a manner that respected both the advances of modern scholarship and earlier tradition.

Methodist Ecclesiologists

We shall now examine the work of various Methodist ecclesiologists within the period up to Methodist Union.

George Gallianders Findlay (1849–1919)

Findlay was a Wesleyan biblical scholar, who spent almost all his ministry in theological training. Most significant of his works for our purposes are a short work on New Testament ecclesiology, *The Church of Christ as set forth in the New Testament* (1893), and his commentary on Ephesians (1900), which is particularly rich in ecclesiological insights.

Findlay represents the confluence of an interesting mixture of influences. His loyalty to the Wesleyan tradition is clearly shown in the following statement: 'There are two things that seem to me most vital to our church life and there is an intimate relation between them – our doctrine of Christian perfection and our doctrine of Christian communion.'[27]

His understanding of the relationship of Church and Kingdom is similar to that of Gregory as is the depth and richness of his ecclesiological vision. In contrast, he held a lower doctrine of the ministry in relationship to the whole people of God than had been the Wesleyan norm. He acknowledged the importance of the ministry as a bond of communion, referring to the 'Church of Christ, compacted in its general framework by those larger ligatures which its ministry furnishes', but there was no stress on the authority of the 'Pastoral Office' as such.[28] Rather, he emphasized the basic equality of people and pastors as disciples. 'The Apostles were disciples first and brethren before they were apostles. They were disciples and brethren to the last.' 'Those who share Peter's confession share his power.' He stated clearly that the ministry arose out of the Church and not vice versa.[29] Most prophetically, for the ecumenical future, Findlay contributed an important christological insight, allowing a balance to be effected between the understanding of 'individual' and 'corporate' salvation. He thereby contributed to the transcending of an important source of division between Protestants and Catholics. He also made an important contribution to the debate on unity in diversity which was not really to come to fruition until almost a century later. Findlay's reading of Ephesians was central to his ecclesiology. He saw the Church as grounded in the trinitarian self-expression of God and his total cosmic design. Picking up Ephesians 2.22, 'a habitation for God in the Spirit', Findlay made much of the Church as God's dwelling place, the central expression of his desire to enter into a relationship with his human creation. He averred:

> The Church is a house built for an Occupant . . . It is built to suit the great inhabitant, who says concerning the new Zion as He said of the old in figure: This is my rest for ever! Here will I dwell, for I have desired it.
>
> God, who is spirit, cannot be satisfied with the fabric of material nature for his temple, nor does 'The Most High dwell in houses made by men's hands'. He seeks our spirit for his abode.

He continues 'In the collective life and spirit of humanity God claims to reside that He may fill it with His glory and His love.'[30] In these statements one has, as it were, the ecclesiological counterpart to St Maximus the Confessor's statement that God willed his 'ensomatiosis' (incarnation) as the culmination of his love for creation.[31]

Like Gregory, Findlay saw the work of the Church within the total cosmic purpose of God. Commenting on Ephesians 3.17–21, he said: 'The Church, being the creation of God's love in Christ . . . is the receptacle of his communicative fullness . . . The life of her people . . . proclaims the Divine goodness, righteousness and truth.' Paul's aim was to see that his readers understand that it was 'the collective aim of Christianity . . . to save humanity and reconstruct the world for a temple of God'. Finally, 'The Church, being the creation of God's love in Christ . . . is the receptacle of his communicative fullness. The life of her people proclaims the Divine goodness, righteousness and truth.'[32]

The relationship of Christ to the Church is particularly related to the risen humanity of the Lord. In his exegesis of Ephesians 1.20–3, Findlay said,

> Again there was poured into the empty, humbled and impoverished form of the Son of God the brightness of the Father's glory and the infinitude of the Father's authority and power. The majesty that He had foregone was restored to Him in undiminished measure! but how great a change meanwhile to Him who received it! This plenitude devolves now not on the Eternal Son in His pure Godhead but on the Christ, the Head and Redeemer of mankind. God . . . has conferred the fullness of all that He is on our Christ . . . He has given Him as replenished and perfected, to the body of His saints, that He may dwell in them and work in them for ever.

Christ and his Church are inseparably united. 'Nor does He render to His Father any tribute in which His people are without a share.' His thought can best be summed up in this concluding quotation:

> She [i.e. the Church] is the vessel of his spirit, the organic instrument of the divine-human life . . . How rich is this gift of the Father to the Church in the Son of His love . . . In the risen and enthroned Christ, God has bestowed on men a gift in which the divine plenitude that fills creation can be embraced.[33]

Perhaps most significant for future ecumenical debate is Findlay's christological distinction between Christ as personal Saviour and 'the Christ' as cosmic redeemer and head of the Church. He derived this distinction from a comparison of Galatians 2.20 where Christ is 'the Son of God who loved me and gave Himself for me' and 'the Christ' of Ephesians 5.23–9, commenting, '*Christ* is the person whom the soul knows and loves, with whom it holds communion in the Spirit. *The Christ* is the same regarded in the wide scope, the Christ of humanity and the ages.'[34]

Findlay was insistent on the interrelationship and interdependence of the individual and the corporate in the Christian life. 'The perfect Christian and the perfect Church are taking shape at once. Each of them requires the other for its realisation.' He refused to talk in terms either of the priority of the community over the individual or the individual over the community, thereby transcending the contrast between 'individual belonging' and 'incorporation' that has been stated, as recently as in the work of Jean-Marie Tillard, to be at the root of the difference between the Catholic and Protestant conceptions of churchly belonging. He referred to individualism as 'negation of the Church's life'.[35] He argued, as did Lidgett a little later, that true personal experience of salvation must issue in a commitment to serve the cosmic purposes of God. Writing of the transition in Paul's own thought between his earlier and later epistles, he commented:

The doctrine of personal salvation wrought out in the great evangelical epistles terminates in that of social and collective salvation . . . the new man is no longer the individual, a mere transformed ego, he is the type and beginning of a new mankind.[36]

Commenting upon Ephesians 3.17–21, he concluded:

Christ came not to save men only but mankind . . . No man in his fragmentary self-hood, no number of men in their separate capacity can conceivably attain to the fullness of God. It will need all of humanity for that. Isolated and divided from one another, we render God a dimmed and partial glory. 'With one accord, with one voice, we are called to glorify the God and father of our Lord Jesus Christ.'[37]

Finally, Findlay had a rich and authentically Wesleyan doctrine of unity in diversity. He argued that this was an apostolic legacy, the apostles having worked 'by methods extremely various'. He continued: 'where there is the same Spirit and the same Lord, men do not need to be scrupulous about visible uniformity'. He contrasted this apostolic catholicism with later concepts of rigid uniformity. Like Beet he made use of the temple metaphor, seeing the various denominational churches as each occupying distinctive rooms within the total structure, their neighbourliness creating a 'web of mutual attachment' until they 'are forgotten in the beauty of the perfect frame. So it will be in the body of Christ, when the several communions, cleansed and filled . . . each honour the vocation of others.'[38] We may see in this an anticipation of the call in the 'Not Strangers But Pilgrims' ecumenical process of the late 1980s to let unity come alive 'by living in one anothers' traditions'.[39]

The value of Findlay's ecclesiology lies above all in his salutary reminder, to a church that had so stressed the importance of an individual experience and appropriation of salvation, of the significance of the complementary truth of God's plan for the corporate redemption and restoration of humankind. In some circles within Methodism, Findlay's ecclesiological insights have yet to be received and acted upon.

Hugh Price Hughes (1847–1902)

Hughes was the single most influential leader in the Wesleyan Methodism of the 1890s, the most active worker for change. He was convinced that Wesleyan Methodism had to make a choice between 'dwindling away into a narrow, feeble stereotyped sect, or growing into a great national Church'.[40] He wanted Methodism to appeal beyond its primarily lower middle-class constituency to a wider range of society, both 'above' and 'below' its previous social parameters. His most recent biographer, Christopher Oldstone-Moore, summarizes his aims for Methodism as fourfold: to create a new style of evangelism, to form a new and wider social conscience, to develop a new social theology and to reform Methodism in a democratic direction.[41] All these aims were linked to his fundamental ecclesiology with

its emphasis upon the 'catholicity' of the Church and his desire
to see that catholicity reflected, as fully as possible, in the life
of Methodism.[42] Inevitably, he came into conflict with such conservatives as Rigg. He did not always get his own way. Nevertheless, he was arguably more responsible than any other individual
for the path taken by early twentieth-century Methodism. He
was the first prominent Methodist to reverse the trend, dating
back to the 1830s, of distancing Methodism further and further
from the Church of England. He also wanted much closer links
with the other free churches. He was an early advocate of
Methodist reunion and was involved in the pioneering ecumenical conversations between Anglicans and free churchmen
that took place at Grindelwald in Switzerland.[43] He recognized
that Methodism needed to rid itself of inherited distortions in
its life and theology. He argued that Wesley's theology had
been over-Pauline and that he had insufficiently addressed the
nature of the Kingdom of God and the importance of Christ
as our example.[44] He contended that later Methodism had
lost much of the original pragmatic flexibility of the early movement and that this adaptability needed to be recovered.[45] Finally,
he was open to the insights of modern thought to a degree
that went way beyond Rigg and the leaders of the previous
generation.

Hughes was not a systematic theologian and his ecclesiology
needs to be teased out from his initiatives and his speeches.
Three things were paramount in it. First came his emphasis,
which was, of course, in accordance with ongoing Wesleyan
tradition, on the true churchliness of any body which, as he put
it, 'showed the unmistakable presence of the miraculous grace
of the Holy Spirit'.[46]

Secondly, he stressed the breadth of the Church's mandate
and function. According to Hughes, a perfect religion must take
account of the individual, the world and God. Transposed into
ecclesiological terms, this meant that the Church must participate fully in national culture and life. While a sect could be
purely inward looking in its concerns, a 'church' 'must be
moulded from without by the principles of the New Testament

and the providential calls of national duty'. Hughes coveted both for Methodism and the other free churches the status of 'churches in the fullest sense, responsible for the spiritual and moral guidance of the whole nation'. Hughes called on nonconformity to emerge from its submerged subcultural status and act as 'the standard bearer of social and political renewal in the Anglo-Saxon world'.[47]

In a sense, Hughes was giving a new orientation to the Methodist mission to 'spread Scriptural holiness throughout the nation'. Previous Methodists had understood this primarily in terms of individual conversion and commitment. Hughes attributed to the Church the duty of campaigning for the adoption of its high ethical standards, so far as practicable, on a national scale.

Thirdly, Hughes was an early advocate of ecumenism. He embraced it because he believed it would give the Church greater power in its campaign for Christian standards in all aspects of social life. He also believed in the catholic destiny of complementary churches. He wished to see the unity of all Protestants, including Anglicans. He believed Anglican and free church strengths dovetailed into each other. Thus, he talked of the possibility that a truly national Christianity 'would be created by the simultaneous movement of non-conformists towards acceptance of social responsibility on the one hand, and, on the other, by the Anglican movement towards the notion of national Christianity as practical righteousness'.[48] He showed more willingness than earlier Wesleyan leaders to take Anglican standpoints seriously into account. Thus, he not merely allowed, as had earlier Wesleyans, that episcopacy was a legitimate form of church government, but even argued that it had been shown to be superior. He contended that it should be accepted as a fact, a fact that had been universal in Christendom from the second to sixteenth centuries.[49] Its acceptance would be inevitable in any really global reunion. In distinguishing between episcopacy as a fact, and any dogma as to its absolute necessity, he laid the ground for much later discussion of the matter both within Methodism and beyond. He reminded Methodists of their liturgical heritage, which, in recent years, had been in danger of attenuation.[50] He defended the idea of a free church catechism, in part because it would demonstrate to the rest of Christendom that the free churches really did understand the importance of doctrine. Hughes was, however, forced to admit that the time was not yet ripe for reunion with the Anglicans. Much of his energy was spent on encouraging free church cooperation. He believed that:

> The zeal and compact organisation of a united Methodism, allied with the intellectualism of Congregationalism, the rugged independence of the Baptists and the lofty spirituality of the Society of Friends, formed an ideal combination which should be endowed throughout with a true sense of their place in the Catholic Church and the heritage that he thought they could claim in it.[51]

The last few words show clearly that, even while apparently concentrating on free church cooperation, Hughes kept in view the wider reality of the Church, within which he saw the free churches as displaying as it were a bundle of 'typoi', or styles, of life and devotion. Hughes was one of the first Methodists to shed the tedious incubus of anti-Catholicism that had characterized so much of Wesleyan Methodism. He contrasted Rome's handling of diversity in styles of mission with that of Protestant churches.

> In Anglicanism . . . or Methodism, or any of the other Protestant communities, if a man comes along full of the zeal of the Holy Ghost, willing . . . to use any method, conventional or unconventional, in the achievement of this purpose, he is scowled at . . . tied up here and tied up there, so that if in the end he wants to do his work in this world he has to clear out . . . But the Pope, on the contrary . . . welcomes him, ties a rope round his waist, and gives him more or less carte blanche to do as he pleases, i.e., he founds an order, and so keeps both himself and the whole concern alive.[52]

Here, perhaps, we have the origin of the idea, later advocated by some Methodist ecumenists, that the destiny of Methodism should be to become an evangelistic order within the wider, reunited Church.

Finally, Hughes was anxious to emphasize that the Church was more than the clergy. He consistently clashed with Rigg and other conservatives in the Wesleyan Church, most particularly over the questions of whether lay persons should participate in the election of the President of the Conference and on the question of whether the representative session of the Conference should have priority over the ministerial. To the accusation that he was erasing the due prerogatives of the ministry, he replied that there should be no sphere of the Church's life in which the laity did not have the right to make their opinions felt.[53]

As has already been stated, Hughes's opinions were not worked out in systematic detail. He cannot be called an ecclesiologist in the sense of Gregory or such later leaders as Flew. Nevertheless, his views, and certainly his attitudes, were arguably more important in shaping the future of Methodism. The reunion of Methodism and its increasing ecumenical openness came about in no small measure because of his efforts.

Joseph Agar Beet (1840–1924)

Agar Beet is perhaps the greatest forgotten theologian of Methodism. Born in 1840, his ministry was almost equally divided between circuit work and teaching at Richmond College where he was deeply appreciated by his students. His desire for absolute candour on difficult aspects of eschatology led him into conflict with some of the notable Wesleyan conservatives of his day and ended with his resigning his position and becoming a supernumerary in 1905.[54]

Beet is best considered as a systematic biblical theologian as opposed to a straight dogmatic theologian like Pope or a biblical commentator such as Findlay. His most distinctive contribution to Wesleyan ecclesiology was in his careful analysis of the biblical metaphors for the Church, though he also threw out some interesting opinions based on his reading of church history.[55] Other Wesleyan ecclesiologists, such as Barrett and Rigg, had concentrated on apologetic for the Wesleyan system; Findlay had stressed the relationship of Christ and the disciples; Flew was to stress the concept of the people of God. The 1937 Statement on the Nature of the Christian Church touched on the metaphors but did not discuss them in detail. Beet, however, dealt with them in some detail, in his *The Church and the Sacraments* of 1907.[56]

Beet's analysis concentrated on five metaphors: the temple, the body, the vine, the flock and the bride. He saw them as balancing emphases upon the divine and human elements in the Church. Thus, he saw the temple metaphor as relating to the active role of the members of the Church in offering praise. 'They [i.e. the Christians] are building their eternal home: and their song will resound for ever.' By contrast, he saw the vine metaphor as relating to the divine energizing of the Church. 'Of this tree, Christ Himself is the root and stem, and the Spirit of God the living and life giving sap, permeating every branch, allowing the branches to live and bear fruit'.[57] The body and bride metaphors relate to the present communion of the Church and to its eschatological vocation and destiny. The body metaphor points to the total communal solidarity of the Church, in which each member and each local church is affected by the help or hindrance of its neighbour. 'The whole Church has one interest. Whatever helps or hinders the spiritual life of an individual is gain or loss to the whole community ... And each church gains or loses by the progress or imperfection of its neighbours.' The bride metaphor emphasizes the eschatological dignity of the Church: 'However unworthy, the chosen object of His tender care ... whom He will cover with His own glory, and make to be partner of His throne'.[58] At the very end of his study of the metaphors, Beet concludes:

The Church on earth has been in all ages and is today the chief agent through which Christ is working out His purposes of mercy to men. And amid forms in great part transient, and marred by many defects, it is a visible anticipation of that all-glorious Church which, without spot or defect will be the eternal Bride of the King of kings.

This eschatological emphasis Beet holds in common with Findlay and Gregory.[59]

In common with Hughes and Findlay, Beet has little to say about the specific traditional Wesleyan concerns of connexionalism and the pastoral office. Like Hughes he is refreshingly free of the traditional anti-Roman Wesleyan line, though he has interesting things to say about Roman Catholic teaching. He rejects the concept of an infallible magisterium alongside that of an infallible Bible; for Beet the outline of fundamental doctrine and experience is sufficiently clear not to need such crutches.[60] He offers a tantalizingly brief thesis that the errors of Rome in regard to the doctrine of the ministry are due to a confusion, from the time of Cyprian onwards, between the status of the Aaronic priesthood and that of the Christian pastorate.[61] This point is of particular interest in view of his sacramental theology where he comes by far the closest to traditional 'Catholic' teaching since the time of the Wesleys. The contrast with earlier Wesleyan ecclesiologists is interesting. Barrett and Gregory scarcely mention the Eucharist. Rigg only mentions it in the context of being the 'seal of church membership'.[62] By contrast, both to his predecessors and to much contemporary free church marginalizing of the sacraments, Beet insists that there is an essential link between eucharistic practice and doctrinal orthodoxy. 'Wherever the rite is performed, the doctrine of salvation through the death of Christ has been firmly held. On the other hand, those who do not hold the doctrine do not know what to do with the rite.'[63] In his *Manual of Theology*, Beet enunciates a form of what would now be called 'eucharistic ecclesiology', emphasizing the Eucharist as 'a means of giving His People corporate and visible unity in the face of the world'.[64] He clearly had a high doctrine of sacramental grace: the sacrament necessarily conveyed grace.

His command makes our reception of the infinite benefits purchased by the death of His Body conditional upon our reception into our bodies of the material bread and wine. Christ has placed these elements of food in unique relationship with Himself ... To the eye of faith, the symbols disappear and the infinite reality alone remains.[65]

In his teaching upon 'eucharistic sacrifice', Beet comes, perhaps surprisingly for a Wesleyan of his era, close to 'Catholic' teaching. While reasserting the normal Protestant point that the Eucharist is never, in the New Testament, called a sacrifice, he argues that its connection with the Jewish Passover reminds us that it is 'in some sense sacrificial action; the analogy of the Jewish and Christian rites is very close'. He continues:

We thus present to God, for our sins, in our hearts and by faith, the pierced body and shed blood of Christ. And while we do so, the blood of Christ saves us from it [sin]. Thus, in the Supper we do a spiritual act analogous to the sprinkling of blood by the High Priest once a year in the Holy Place.

But since we do but present to God as a propitiation for our sins the blood already shed once for all, it is better to call the Supper a sacrificial act rather than a sacrifice.[66]

Here, perhaps, we see Beet struggling towards the modern concept of the biblical memorial. Had he held a stronger concept of 'sacramental sign', he might have arrived at it before such later scholars as Max Thurian.[67]

Other features of Beet's ecclesiology are his doctrine of development and his understanding of unity in diversity. The former clearly emerges in an aside on the 'restorationism' of the Plymouth Brethren.

The growth and experience of the centuries are too precious to set aside. To the Christian life existing at our birth, we owe our knowledge and our spiritual life. However, the outward forms of the earliest churches are as unfit for present needs as are the clothes of childhood to a full grown man. The Gospel is a life, not a prescription ... to ignore the developments of the past is to throw away the hope of healthy development in the future.[68]

Beet believed that the Church had been enriched by the 'happy fault' of divisions and the resultant separate developments. He also believed that 'no church had ever prospered with individual sway', that is, when it enjoyed an ecclesial monopoly, but he did not believe that disunity had to prevail for all time. Thus, he asserted:

> Different churches embody different types of spirituality, and the types are a lesson and enrichment to the whole ... The divisions caused or made needful by sin are God's way of purifying His Church and leading it to higher and richer unity. And in many cases it is expedient that the outward forms be retained till the types therein embodied have been appropriated by other communions.[69]

This teaching seems to be similar to that in the recent papal encyclical, *Ut Unum Sint*, where Pope John Paul II teaches that there has been a 'rich embellishment' of the *koinonia* arising out of the divisions of Christendom. This now needs to be re-received and shared within restored communion.[70]

It is a pity that Beet did not write more fully on ecclesiology. The few suggestions he threw out show considerable independence of mind and anticipation of later ecumenical ecclesiology.

John Scott Lidgett (1854–1953)

Lidgett has been regarded by some as the most remarkable Methodist minister since the time of Wesley. Entering the ministry in 1876, he remained active in the work till 1948. Much of his work was produced not in the relative leisure of an academic appointment but amid the hurly-burly of his ministry at the Bermondsey Mission. From the ecclesiological point of view, his most important works are his commentary on Ephesians, *God in Christ Jesus* (1915), and his collection of essays of 1927, *God, Christ and the Church*, the last third of which is devoted to ecumenically orientated ecclesiology. He was President of the Wesleyan Conference in 1908 and President of the Uniting Conference in 1932. His influence on Methodist social thinking, practice of mission and ecumenical activity was profound.[71]

Though Hughes must probably be considered the pioneer of modern Methodist ecumenism, Lidgett was the first Methodist scholar both to contribute to and to assimilate the insights of the early modern ecumenical movement. He was more open to non-Wesleyan theological traditions than earlier Methodist leaders.[72]

Fundamental for an appreciation of his ecclesiological presuppositions is his commentary on Ephesians. Basic to his whole theology was his understanding of the fatherhood of God, 'the climax and ultimate explanation of all religion' and 'the only hope of catholicity'.[73] Its corporate and ecclesiological implications are clear in the following quotation:

> The purpose of the Father is to reveal His love in the incarnate life of His eternal Son and to make possible the sharing of that life in a thoroughly filial relationship with all humankind ... God has planted an infinite receptivity in the heart of man to correspond with His eternal purpose to impart His own infinite perfection as the gift of His holy Love.[74]

According to Lidgett, God's final aim is the fulfilment of all the latent potential for creative relationship that the Father has planned for humankind.

This emphasis on the corporate destiny of humankind naturally impinges on both Lidgett's Christology and ecclesiology. He argued that, in the catholicity of God's purpose, individuals were 'differentiated yet held together'. Since that purpose is 'inescapably social and universal, there is no such thing as a purely personal sonship of God, existing apart from the life of human fellowship'.[75] In an interesting reassertion of a point made by Gregory, and in anticipation of the thought of the modern Orthodox theologian John Zizioulas, Lidgett argues that 'without the Church, Christ is unfulfilled'.[76] His primacy as transcendent head of the Church is only fulfilled in his immanence within it and his communication of his divine energy to it. In turn, the Church is not 'complete in itself', but exists as the necessary sphere of God's working towards the consummation of the Kingdom for all humanity. Central to an understanding of this is the contemplation of the great mystery of the union of Jew and Gentile in the Church, sign of its outreaching inclusivity.[77]

In his understanding of the unity of the Church as a developing process, Lidgett is at one with Gregory.

The Apostle [i.e. in Ephesians] describes unity as the goal rather than the starting point ... [he] is able to take for granted a certain measure of unity at the outset. But it is inchoate, and can only be fulfilled and made perfect by the spiritual development that gives full control to the head. Only growth into the head can accomplish this.[78]

Unity is to be built through the reception of the power and grace of the Christ who indwells his Church.

For Lidgett in 1915, as for Gregory over forty years previously, unity can only come through the vitality of grace. He describes unity as 'vital rather than institutional'. The attainment of unity results from 'the vital interpenetration of Christ and His members', and can only be restored, after rupture, by 'a common growth into Christ ... in the mutual receptiveness and service that can only come from perfecting in love'.[79] At this stage, Lidgett shared much of the traditional Wesleyan distrust of emphasis upon specific structures at the expense of the enlivening Spirit. He states that 'organisation is unfruitful and even dangerous apart from life'.[80] The 1920s were to see him taking a more positive attitude to the view that the Church needs a universally accepted and acceptable ministry of *koinonia*.[81]

In his presidential charge of 1908, and again in *God in Christ*

Jesus, Lidgett's doctrine of the ordained ministry is couched neither in traditional Wesleyan terms of the 'Pastoral Office', nor yet in terms of a ministry of connexion and *koinonia*. Rather, to use a now increasingly popular ecumenical concept, it is seen in terms of a 'ministry of memory', of reminding the Church of the abiding centrality of its universal vocation. The ministry of the great apostle Paul is paradigmatic in terms of its awakening of people to the cosmic dimension of God's great plan. It was, above all, a ministry of memory and of eschatological vision, constantly reminding the Church alike of its call and its glorious promised destiny.[82]

Like many others of his generation, Lidgett was profoundly influenced by the setting up of the League of Nations after the end of World War I. He did not want the churches to miss out on their chance to shape progressive developments in international relationships, but feared their disunity might stymie them. However, he also argued that reunion of the churches could never take place solely for the sake of meeting an external situation: 'it can only come to pass as a common faith demands common expression . . . and as the need for closer and wider fellowship cries out for it'.[83] Unity must grow out of the imperatives inherent in ecclesial awareness, the most important of which is the need to allow for the full development of the 'catholic potential of the Church'. Lidgett believed that this could not happen except in the context of lived, organic *koinonia*. His sense of the richness of the varying gifts of the different denominations, and of their need for complementary fulfilment by others, received a new strength in the post-war world.

Moreover the one life of the Spirit, being heavenly, universal and catholic in nature, cannot be developed to perfection in national or sectional communities. All denominations, Roman, Eastern and Anglican as well as nonconformist, speak provincial dialects, which betray their lack of fulfilled catholicity. It is imperative that these provincialisms should be transcended, if the fullness of the 'truth as it is in Jesus' is to be reached. And this communion can only be brought about in and through one communion, with its corporate organisation and life. Such catholicity as belongs to each denomination, be it more or less, can only be preserved in so far as it energises in pursuit of more.[84]

This last statement is particularly interesting as an ecclesiological deduction, in the spirit of Gregory, from the doctrine of Christian perfection. A church which does not 'press on to full salvation' and 'further imaging of the Kingdom' imperils its very catholicity.

Lidgett's emphasis upon the fatherhood of God and the resultant brotherhood of mankind can seem, at first sight, rather sentimentally Liberal Protestant. It must, however, be seen within the context of his very exacting concept of the fatherly demands of God, which are anything but easy and sentimental.[85] It is also clear, from Lidgett's later commendation of and commentary upon a central passage in the Lambeth Appeal of 1920, that he saw the catholic vocation to unity as demanding a spiritually exacting process of mutual reception of gifts on the part of sister churches.[86] For Lidgett, unity was essential to the credibility of the gospel. 'Surely, the condition . . . of successful evangelism is that the condition of the Church should be in full correspondence with the reality in which it lives and to which it witnesses.'[87] The Church, thus, is not the mere purveyor of the message; it necessarily embodies it. To cite Lidgett yet again:

Yet the credentials of the Church are rejected and its ministry neglected because our unhappy divisions prevent us from having one mind, speaking with one voice and manifesting the glory of a sacrifice that has attained its full vigour by triumphing over the most insidious forms of faction and self-seeking . . . the cause of Christ is at stake. It can only be saved by the answer to His own prayer that they all may be one.[88]

Here, we have an interesting ecclesiological insight that, in the setting aside of self-seeking on the part of its varied denominations, the Church offers a corporately filial response, in Christ, to the Father, a response that helps to authenticate its message. The search for unity can, thus be seen as a sort of corporate 'spiritual sacrifice' (Rom. 12.22), encapsulating, as it were, the fullness of a kenotic response by the Church to the will of the Father.

Lidgett's understanding of the relationship of the Church to the Kingdom constitutes the second pole of his ecclesiology. He anticipated much that has been said on this subject in more recent ecumenical ecclesiology. However, he argues that the Church is more than just the instrument of the Kingdom, calling it also the *immediate* sphere of Christ's kingship. He states:

> The Church is a living organism, the development of which is by way of complete fellowship towards the perfect realis-ation of the Divine relationships in and for which it has its being. Hence, it is by its nature and constitution equivalent to the Kingdom and manifests it so far as the Kingdom itself has, as yet, been spiritually realised.

He went on to assert that the Church:

> though a distinct organism and organisation, is not self-contained and cut off from the rest of mankind, which is to be gathered into the Kingdom by being brought to the enjoy-ment of those Divine relations of life and love into which believers have already entered by virtue of their restored and fulfilled Sonship. Hence there is the prospect of a three fold fulfilment – of Christ's kingdom, of His Church . . . and of mankind brought through the grace of Christ and the ministry of the Church to the full enjoyment of the life of the Father . . . and these three are one.[89]

Lidgett's summary of the relationship of Church and Kingdom seems to go beyond the 'sign, instrument and first fruits' of later ecumenical dialogue. It points to a particularly subtle concept of the convergence of Church, Kingdom and destiny of human-kind as necessarily related to each other and interdependent.

Perhaps the nearest analogue to Lidgett's thought is in the theologoumenon of the contemporary Catholic ecumenist, George Tavard, who talks of the Church as 'progressively imaging' the Kingdom.[90] The relationship that Lidgett posited did not fit the contemporary continental Protestant emphasis upon the Kingdom as utterly transcendent and unrelated to any human endeavour whatsoever. Rather, in the spirit of Arminianism and a belief in what modern American Methodist theologians call 'responsible grace', a vision is given that integrates divine initiative and human response alike. Lidgett argues:

> Any conceivable kingdom of Christ must rest upon and develop certain spiritual relations between Christ and His people, and ultimately between God in Christ, on the one hand, and mankind as represented by Christ's people on the other. However we may magnify Divine Grace, Spiritual Power and Sovereign Activity, the way in which these work must be determined by the end towards which they are directed and the sphere in which they operate. And these are to be found in the spirit of man, as destined to the fellowship and service of God.[91]

Lidgett was well aware of the distortions that an over-individualistic emphasis on salvation had created within the Protestant churches. He reinforced his earlier emphasis on the necessary link between individual faith and corporate belonging. To the assertion that individual faith was primary and ecclesial belonging of very secondary importance, Lidgett riposted: 'It is true that faith is personal . . . yet just because it is personal, it is extremely social, not individualistic. It is self-communicative and lives by sharing and not in isolation.'[92] Faith in and acceptance of the Father's plan and design necessarily orientated the one who came to faith towards participation in the grand catholic design of God, and thus necessarily implied ecclesial belonging. Lidgett's understanding of this appears clearly in his treatment both of Tradition and of development in the Church. He stressed the 'collective witness of the Church' as the 'great inheritance which it has received'. The watchword of faith and prophecy should be 'other men have laboured and you have entered into their labours'.[93] He maintained a strong defence of the value and necessity of the traditional credal formulations of the Church against those free churchmen who were inclined to doubt their value. However, he also kept a fine balance between emphasis on the value of Tradition and stress on the possibility of future progressive development of understanding in faith. He regarded freedom in theological thought as essential to the latter. 'To achieve unity at the expense of freedom would, therefore, cut the nerve of spiritual progress.'

> Reunion must be so constituted as not to crystallise the past, but to set forth the belief that you best preserve the truth by going on more fully to describe it. It must find plenty of room not merely for the priest but for the prophet.[94]

Lidgett's sheer breadth of spiritual and ecumenical vision can perhaps best be illustrated from his remarks at the end of a comparative study of Wesley and Newman which formed the closing chapter of *God, Christ and the Church*.[95] He posed the question of the possibility of an ultimate reconciliation of their insights, commenting:

> Some say that this is impossible, and that the religion of the Spirit and the Religion of Authority must for ever confront one another in unreconciled antagonism ... Yet if, as we have seen, the oppositions take their rise in differences of emphasis and selection out of the vast realm of spiritual experience, may there not come a time when the birth of a new and more comprehensive spirit, informed by fuller knowledge and with a wider outlook, may transcend them both in a larger apprehension and interpretation of Christ.[96]

In such an opinion, Lidgett showed himself well in advance of other Methodists, such as his eminent near-contemporary, Henry Bett. Bett, in his *Spirit of Methodism*, still regarded the 'experientialism' of Methodism and the 'traditionalism' of Roman Catholicism as irreconcilable.[97]

As a good 'son in the Gospel' of Mr Wesley, Lidgett was well aware that God works both through the ongoing traditional institutions of the Church and through prophetic charisms, including those of 'irregular' ministers, raised up from time to time to supply what others could or would not do. In his later, inter-war ecumenical work, Lidgett combined both 'Wesleyan' and 'catholic' insights into the question of ministerial order. He distinguished between the necessity of episcopacy for a fully reunited Church, as the form of order most widely acceptable, and episcopacy as not necessary per se to genuine churchliness.[98] He accepted the vital role played historically by the episcopate in maintaining the faith and building up the bonds of *koinonia* in the early Church, while warning against exclusive ideas of ministry as betraying a static concept of the Church. He argued that the Church needed to grow and preserve its identity by 'such ordered change as promotes a fuller expression of life'. It was in this context that he commended the Lambeth Appeal of 1920.[99]

In line with his understanding of the relationship between Church and Kingdom, Lidgett had a strong sense of the eschatological destiny of the Church. Ephesians 4 is central to his ecclesiology. He held that the dynamic ecclesiology of the mystical Body of Christ there expounded necessarily implied the search for unity.

> The Apostle treats the full attainment of unity as the result, or at least the concomitant and mark, of maturity . . . catholic unity is, therefore, the immanent ideal of the Church's life, but the full realisation . . . in the future must be the product of all the forces that make for fellowship, completed in perfect faith and the full knowledge of the Son of God.

Growth in holiness and unity are interdependent.

> I take it that this (Eph. 4.13) means that unity can only be fulfilled as we come to the more intimate knowledge of Christ

and that all such knowledge of Christ must of necessity tend to the complete organisation of unity on earth.[100]

Lidgett had no truck with the argument that organic unity was unnecessary because true believers were already 'spiritually' united. He held that the very awareness of spiritual unity constrained those conscious of it to seek for its 'bodily expression', since 'the one life of the Spirit cannot be developed to its perfection in national or sectional communities'.[101] He balanced an acceptance of the fact that new truths could indeed be developed in separation with an emphasis that this did not constitute a case for the maintenance of the evil of separation.

In many respects, Lidgett's ecclesiology was ahead of his times, particularly his Methodist times. Methodism, in general, was absorbed with the question of its own reunion. Nevertheless, as early as the thirties, Methodists were acknowledging that the 'coming Great Church' would include episcopal, presbyteral and congregational elements.[102] Perhaps no Methodist theologian, other than Geoffrey Wainwright at a later stage, has done so much to assimilate and commend to Methodists the insights of the wider Ecumenical Movement.[103] Along, perhaps, with Gregory, Lidgett is the ecclesiologist whom Methodists need most to 're-receive' today.

Arthur Samuel Peake (1865–1929)

Peake is most remembered as a biblical scholar and as a major influence on the adjustment of Primitive Methodism to the challenges and opportunities of modern critical scholarship.[104] However, his influence on ecclesiological and ecumenical thought was also liberating, positive and considerable. From student days, he was devoted to the cause of organic unity. He remained, however, a deeply convinced free churchman. His biographer commented that, alongside 'the widest ecumenical interests, there was never any deviation from free church principles, as he understood them, which he strongly upheld'. He insisted, however, that he was a high churchman and that the only antidote to 'high clericalism' (as he called the exaggerated exaltation of the prerogatives of the ordained ministry) was a high doctrine of the Church. He would not concede 'the dominance of the two sacraments' over other and non-sacramental means of grace, but he was prepared to accept a 'constitutional episcopacy' within a reunited Church. He was extraordinarily sensitive to the opinions of others, however much they might differ from those of his own tradition. 'Our first duty to those separated from us is not to refute them but to understand them. Of all the qualities in this connection that of a sympathetic imagination is most to be prized.' As a free churchman he made known his principled opposition to 'establishment', but he wished to see it gradually eroded by reform promoted from within the Church of England or in the general political process rather than by free church agitation which might only embitter Anglicans. Peake's was an ecumenical spirit in the best sense, one prepared to engage with the real concerns of others rather than to ignore or attempt to refute them.[105] His combination of loyalty to his own tradition and genuine empathy with others remains an example to all ecumenists.

The 1937 Statement: 'Nature of the Christian Church'

Finally, we turn to the 1937 Conference statement, 'Nature of the Christian Church'. In 1935, the Conference of the newly reunited Methodist Church had created a 'Faith and Order' committee, largely to help it respond adequately to questions posed by the faith and order wing of the ecumenical movement. The three separate, uniting churches had each been represented at the Lausanne Faith and Order Conference of 1927; another world 'Faith and Order' Conference was scheduled for Edinburgh in 1937. With this in mind, the Conference directed the new committee to draft a statement on the nature of the Church as understood in Methodism.[106]

The draft was duly debated and adopted at the Conference of 1937. It constituted the first comprehensive ecclesiological statement issued by British Methodism. The Conference did not

aim at adopting an exclusively confessionally Methodist document, nor did it wish to impose a straightjacket on subsequent
Methodist ecclesiology. Rather, it recognized the need for ecclesiological debate and discussion within both Methodism and the
wider Church. It aimed also to give theological backing to the
ecclesiological claims of the Deed of Union and to recover for
Methodists a sense of reverence for the Church as the Body of
Christ and to promote Methodist reflection on such questions.
The Conference of 1938, after hearing of the wide-ranging
debates on Church, Ministry and Sacraments at Edinburgh, recognized that there could be little progress on these particularly
difficult issues until there was prior agreement on the nature of
the Church.[107]

The 1937 Report clearly bore the imprint of Robert Newton
Flew, tutor at Wesley House, the Methodist theological college
at Cambridge, a leading New Testament scholar and contemporary British Methodism's leading ecumenical statesman. The
report needs to be read in conjunction with Flew's magisterial
work on the ecclesiology of the New Testament, *Jesus and His
Church*, a work that, in itself, represented the most substantial
Methodist work of formal ecclesiology since Gregory's *Holy
Catholic Church* of 1873.[108] Flew wrote it, in part, to scout
the idea, then fashionable among some radical New Testament
scholars, that the concept of the Church had no roots in the
mind or ministry of Jesus but was purely a post-resurrection
development. The central chapter of the first half of the book
examines in detail 'the idea of the ecclesia in the mind of Our
Lord'.[109] Flew was determined to show that the Church was
central and integral to Christianity, not an optional after-
thought. Other studies have since clarified aspects of New Testament ecclesiology, but none has fully replaced Flew's magisterial
contribution.

The Statement represents a maturing of the Methodist ecclesiological tradition, both in terms of its own internal development
and in terms of the relationship with the ecumenical movement.
It presents (though in less detail), as Lidgett had done earlier, a
grand vision of the nature of the Church in the overall design of

God.[110] It echoes many of the insights of the classical Wesleyan theologians, while eschewing their confrontational tone. Its major omission was any serious consideration of 'connexionalism', then still seen purely as a Methodist 'peculiar institution' rather than as a matter for ecumenical discussion.

A delicate balance is maintained between the classical Methodist emphasis on the missionary mandate of the Church, as addressed to every *individual*, and the corporate call of the Church to transform every sphere of human life and achievement. Thus, we are told that, in New Testament times, 'the individual experience was never severed in thought from membership in the Christian community' and that 'the process of claiming for Christ every activity of the Christian man and redeeming every department of the corporate life of the world began in those New Testament days'. Personal religion is set in the forefront, but also in the context of preparing for the goal and consummation of history.[111]

The Statement was more systematic than anything produced by earlier individual Wesleyan ecclesiologists. It dealt with important questions of hermeneutics, of fundamental ecclesiology and doctrinal development, relating these to the particular insights and emphases of the Methodist tradition. Thus, in describing the biblical images of the Church, it says,

> All the metaphors are modes of describing that which is real, even if ultimately undescribable – that relationship to God, so intimate and undeserved, which God has established with those that he has called to walk with him. *The decisive element in the New Testament conception of the Church is the presence of the living Christ in the midst of his own.*[112]

This last statement is clearly linked to the Methodist experiential emphasis. It coheres with that spelt out rather more fully by Flew in his book of 1938.

> The Word of God which called the Church into existence has been verified in human experience. Thus Christians were

already acting in the proud consciousness that they are the
new Israel . . . Already the divinely given principle of fellowship in the Holy Spirit is being translated into the life of the
new community.[113]

The Statement argues that the life of the Church develops ever
more fully with each succeeding age.

The Church of Christ is the home of the Holy Spirit, and is
therefore a family with a unique and developing life. It is a
life of distinctive quality, a life which under the guidance of
the Holy Spirit should be richer as time goes on, with fresh
manifestations as new nations and new races are added to
the Church and new apprehension of divine truth is given.[114]

As in the thought of Findlay, a careful balance is maintained
between emphasis upon the corporate vocation of the Church
and the importance of individual salvation. 'Personal religion is
set in the forefront. The Church exists for the conversion of
sinners and the multiplying and perfecting of the saints.' In the
same paragraph we read, 'That purpose [i.e. of the Church] is
to prepare the way for the goal and consummation of all history,
the final coming of the rule or kingdom of God, which has
already been manifested in the redemptive activity of Christ.'
The axis upon which this takes place is God's plan of reconciliation, effected in Christ, joining Jew and Gentile across the
age-old barrier.[115]

Out of a divided humanity God created a new and united
humanity in Christ. This is the beginning of a world-wide
process of reconciliation, which will only be complete when
all things are brought into submission to the rule of God.[116]

The paradoxical nature of ecclesial existence is nuanced. The
visible Church is called 'an imperfect and fallible instrument of
God's will', a statement that is balanced by the observation,
relating to the biblical images of the Church, that 'ideal as they

may seem ... there are realities behind them'. The Church is
simultaneously the object of God's grace and the imperfect
instrument of his will. The temptations of 'monophysite' and
'nestorian' ecclesiology are alike eschewed. The Church has its
inseparable divine and human elements. Neither is swallowed
up in the other.[117]

It is important to stress that the Statement is quite clear on
the visible nature of the Church.

> The reality denoted is both visible and spiritual. It is visible
> because it is grouped in various local communities. It is spir-
> itual because the call which has gathered them and the gift
> of the Spirit which they share, the allegiance by which they
> are bound, the destiny to which they move – all these are not
> of this world. They are not of man's contrivance but of God's
> gift.

The emphasis upon the visibility in the local community is not,
however, fully developed in the Statement.[118]

It is the Pentecostal experience of the Spirit that is at the
centre of the ecclesiology of the 1937 Report. It is seen as
determining the worshipping life and the structures of the
Church.

> The common experience *issued in common worship* and this
> is expressed in the two sacraments of the baptism and the
> Lord's Supper, in prayer, in preaching, and in the social activi-
> ties of love. This experience is seen as given to all the gathered
> believers on the day of Pentecost and not just to the Eleven
> who then transmitted it to others.[119]

In *Jesus and His Church*, Flew echoes an emphasis of Agar
Beet's upon the 'democratization' of the Spirit, in contrast to
the Old Covenant, where the Spirit fell only on certain specially
chosen people. This understanding did not, however, preclude
the belief that special gifts are given to those chosen as the
ministers of the Church. It did not mean that the community

should be unstructured. Fellowship was 'the inward bond which necessarily called for the outward acts in which it can be expressed'. A ministry of *koinonia* is one such, a point that is implicit, but not spelt out, in the Report.[120]

From these principles, in association with the overall purpose of the Church in God's total design, derives the Methodist understanding of catholicity and apostolicity. The true catholicity of the Church is to be found in its mandate and task. The mandate is nothing less than the evangelization of every person and the redemption of humankind in all its relationships. The quality of the catholicity of the Church rests upon its fidelity to these tasks. Any retreat into sectarianism or world-renouncing piety impairs that catholicity. Catholicity also relates to recognition. The implication is that the failure to recognize the ecclesial reality of a sister church of a differing tradition which holds to the essentials of the faith and the universal mission would impair the catholicity of the Church. This implication is clearly in the tradition of Benjamin Gregory. It is also linked with the recognition that, in separation, the churches are likely to fail to achieve a fully rounded understanding of their nature and task. Distortions will inevitably result. In these statements, a doctrine of 'reception' is implied but not spelt out.[121] The apostolicity of the Church is seen as residing most particularly in the 'continuity of Christian experience'. The whole Church shares in the 'binding and loosing power that was granted to Peter as the first of many to confess the Christ through whom liberation from sin, and salvation, came. 'Those who share Peter's faith, share his power' (The Report, quoting Findlay). Apostolicity is not dependent upon a particular form of ministerial succession. It is, rather, manifested in the continued acceptance of the Apostolic Faith, the 'fundamental principles of the historic creeds' and the celebration of the two gospel sacraments.[122]

The Statement's definition of apostolicity anticipated later ecumenical thinking about it as a whole bundle of characteristics of churchly life rather than as primarily based upon or dependent upon the one strand of ministerial succession. Its exact formulation, in 1937, was influenced by the continuing Methodist dispute with the Tractarian tradition. The approach taken to it in the Statement is not well integrated with its treatment either of the ministry or the overall purpose of the Church. It might have been improved by some consideration as to how the ministry, rather than any one particular form of it is, nevertheless, integral to the continuing apostolicity of the Church.[123]

A carefully nuanced statement on the ministry is, nevertheless, given in the Report. It is seen as arising within the Church while yet being a *gift* to it. The teaching of 1 Corinthians 12 is held to imply the former and that of Ephesians 4 the latter. The two views are held to be complementary and not contradictory. Ministry is 'created by the Spirit', ministries being 'given by the glorified Lord to the Church for the building up of the Body of Christ', but organized by the Church. Ministry and Church are in a symbiotic relationship. Ministry is not a purely human creation, nor yet does it exist independently of the Church; rather, it exists *within* the Church.[124]

The 1937 Report concludes with an exposition of the principles of the Deed of Union concerning the doctrinal standards of Methodism and its place within the Universal Church. It enunciates the 'principles of the Protestant Reformation as threefold, viz. – salvation by faith, the mediatorship of Christ, and the priesthood of all believers'. They are seen as a 'rediscovery of the heart of the Gospel'. The intention here is to safeguard the Methodist emphasis upon the *immediate* relationship of the believer to Christ (in contrast to any idea that this can only be mediated by sacramental grace, the availability even of that depending upon the 'orders' of the minister of the sacraments). However, the immediate relationship of the believer with Christ is seen as always implying a coordinate ecclesial belonging and participation, an emphasis we have already noted in Findlay's ecclesiology.[125]

Finally, the Statement emphasizes that 'Methodists can never surrender the conviction that the Evangelical Revival of the eighteenth century was the work of God.' This assertion is carefully prefaced by a nuanced analysis of the ambiguities inherent in the rise of Methodism. It is accepted that the Wesleys never wanted their movement to separate from the Church of England. At the same time, it is also argued that the societies were never an integral part of the Church of England, and that to talk of 'separation' from Anglicanism 'without far reaching qualifications' would be incorrect. The attitude of many Anglicans forced Wesley to work outside the structures of the established church. Methodism was 'guilty of no schism'.[126] Notwithstanding this, Methodism did not rest content with the divided state of Christendom, but pledged itself wholeheartedly to work for reunion.[127]

The 1937 Statement provided a broad and finely nuanced ecclesiological statement, tailored both to the perceived needs of the Connexion and the wider contemporary ecclesiological debate. Following the dying down of old intra-Methodist disputes, and the much closer association with the other free churches, it ignored the specifically Methodist insight of 'connexionalism'. Despite this last lacuna, the Report served Methodism well for over half a century and its enduring worth was reaffirmed within the working party that was eventually charged to draft a successor report in the 1990s.

4

Called to Love and Praise

The 1937 statement 'Nature of the Christian Church' represented the climax of an era in Methodist ecclesial consciousness. It came at the end of a period which saw Methodism, more especially Wesleyan Methodism, emerge from the ecclesial ghetto in which it had cocooned itself from the early years of the nineteenth century till the 1890s. In that period, the main branches of British Methodism had negotiated and achieved reunion. Methodism had also entered into close relationships with the other free churches. In the later part of the period, Methodist relations with the Church of England had improved to a degree and Methodism had become fully involved in the infant ecumenical movement. The period was also characterized by a shift to a markedly more liberal theological position. Few Methodists now refused to acknowledge the importance of modern biblical scholarship. It had therefore been logical that the report 'Nature of the Christian Church', intended, at least in part, as a contribution towards the contemporary ecumenical faith and order debate, had set out an understanding of the Church that stressed both a modern comprehension of relevant New Testament teaching and a Methodist position on key contemporary ecumenical issues.

Sixty-two years were to elapse before another fully rounded ecclesiological statement, approved by the Conference, was to appear. During this period theological issues were raised and Faith and Order statements approved by the Conference which clearly had ecclesiological relevance. This was particularly true of the statements on ordination of 1960 and 1974.[1] In another sense, however, there was remarkably little attention given to fundamental ecclesiology in itself. One might have expected more fundamental ecclesiology to emerge from the Anglican–Methodist conversations of the 1960s. Some important ecclesiological points were made in the ensuing controversies and one excellent book on the Methodist ecclesiological tradition, Rex Kissack's *Church or No Church*, was written in 1964. In it, he drew attention to the neglected riches of nineteenth-century Wesleyan ecclesiology, particularly those of Gregory. Kissack reasserted Gregory's emphases upon apostolic recognition and visible unity. He made some valuable remarks upon infallibility and indefectibility and criticized the lacunae both of the 'catholic' approach to ecumenism and the 'federalist' approach of many free church people. Generally, however, attention was focused almost entirely on the nature and status of the ministry within the Church as an ecumenical question rather than upon the fundamental question of the nature and purpose of the Church in itself. In this, Methodism represented a tendency, evident elsewhere, to discuss the nature of ministry as a 'given', rather isolated from its ecclesiological context. In this respect, the 1980s and 1990s saw a welcome shift throughout the Christian world, with questions of ministry and apostolicity being placed more securely within a fuller ecclesiological context.[2]

Perhaps one reason for the failure of the Anglican–Methodist Conversations of the 1950s and 1960s was a failure to appreciate the need for a carefully nuanced and properly defended ecclesiology to undergird all the proposals that were made about the reconciliation and integration of ministries and the ultimate organic union of the two churches.

Alongside changes in the ecumenical situation came sea changes in theological method and denominational self-confidence in comparison with the 1930s. Then, most people had assumed both the existence of a clear-cut biblical theology and a set of denominational positions on key ecclesiological issues that would remain constant.[3] These gave way, under the impact of post-war emphases on diversity, postmodernism and contextuality, to a degree of relativism in which nothing seemed as simple as it had once done.[4] One of the interesting and admirable features of the 1999 ecclesiology report, entitled *Called to Love and Praise*, was that it achieved a delicate balance between acknowledging the new developments and the questions they posed and maintaining a modified, but still distinctively Methodist, understanding of the place of Scripture and Tradition.[5]

The working party of the Faith and Order Committee that met in 1990 to consider the issuing of a new report in ecclesiology began by considering the enormous changes that had occurred since 1937. There was considerable hesitation about the relationship of the new report to the 1937 statement. Should it be seen as superseding it or merely as complementing it? Generally, the 1937 report was respected for its clarity and achievement, but, as *Called to Love and Praise* itself eventually stated:

> The very different situation of the Church in the 1990s warrants a new statement. This does not mean that the earlier statement must now be contradicted, but simply that there are new things to be said in a context very different from that of sixty years ago.[6]

The working party further specified that: 'Christians, called to respond to the Creator's concern for the healing and unity of the world, must ask what the Church is and what it is for.'[7]

Major developments in ecumenism and in biblical scholarship were seen as two key factors compelling ecclesiological reassessment.[8] Both ecumenical dialogue and local ecumenical cooperation had made immense strides since 1937. Methodism had become involved in several bilateral international theological dialogues and in the multilateral 'Baptism, Eucharist, Ministry' Process of the World Council of Churches. Locally, Methodists were also involved in many joint URC/Methodist churches, to say nothing of the many other Local Ecumenical Partnerships.[9] The closer links with other churches had both provided new ecclesiological insights and enabled the separate denominations to see their own distinctive features in clearer perspective. The sections of the Report on *koinonia*, on the four fundamental 'notes' of the Church and on the distinctively Methodist understanding and experience of the Church bear witness to the reception of these insights by the working party, subsequently endorsed by the Conference.[10] The 1937 Report had been content with a relatively brief assertion of Methodist catholicity and some account of Methodist origins: the 1999 Report gave a very full account of Methodist self-understanding and an ecclesiological interpretation of its structures.[11]

Where Scripture was concerned, the position of the 1999 Report was much more nuanced than that of the 1937 one. Then, it had been assumed that there was a fundamental New Testament ecclesiology to which Methodism adhered, rejecting any biblically unsupported claims of later 'tradition' concerning, for example, the essential nature of the episcopal succession for ecclesial integrity. Such a stance was in harmony with the then very recent statement of the Deed of Union concerning the 'Divine revelation recorded in the Holy Scriptures' as the 'supreme rule of faith and practice'.

By the 1990s both biblical scholarship and its ecumenical reception had moved on. To the nineteenth-century Wesleyan insight that Scripture prescribed no one system of church order or ministry as such was now added a new understanding of the complexity of the relationship between Scripture and Tradition. This reflected the enormous amount of work on the subject at and after the Montreal Faith and Order Conference of 1963. Both this and the importance of 'contextualization' were acknowledged in *Called to Love and Praise*. The Report gave a finely nuanced statement on the relationship of Scripture, Tradition and experience. This, in turn, reflected both developments within the understanding of the Wesleyan tradition and developments in ecumenical theology and biblical interpretation. *Called to Love and Praise* acknowledged the symbiotic relationship of Scripture and Tradition 'in dialogue'. 'The tradition is the context which shapes our use of Scripture, and Scripture is the resource by which the tradition is deepened and purified.'[12] Scripture was seen as the most dependable of all witnesses to

Christ. However, the authority of Christ was distinguished from any simple identification with Scripture, a point consistent with the teaching of the Deed of Union which had talked of 'the Divine revelation recorded in the Holy Scriptures'. Experience was seen as having a key 'confirmatory role'. These two tightly argued paragraphs revealed a welding together of the emphases of the Deed of Union, the reassessment of the Wesleyan 'quadrilateral' by Albert Outler and others, and the advances made at Montreal and elsewhere on Scripture, Tradition and teaching authority.[13]

Linked with the discussion of the Scripture–Tradition problem was a discussion of the question of authority. Three points were made. The first was that the supreme authority is Christ, to whom there are dependable witnesses, most especially Scripture. The second was that walking by faith and not sight in this life implied that 'absolute or infallible authorities are not immediately available'. Finally, it was stressed that experience, 'nurtured, stimulated and corrected by the witness of Scripture and Tradition', helps to 'confirm the truth that is in Christ' and gives 'sufficient light by which to travel'.[14]

One may observe that this discussion of authority is tantalizingly short, given the very considerable ecumenical orientation of the report and the significance that the question of authority has in current ecumenical debate.[15] Nevertheless, one of the undoubted strengths of the report, in general, was the way in which ecumenical concerns were addressed at almost every juncture rather than being confined to a specifically ecumenical section.

Called to Love and Praise was defined as having four key purposes. First, to help Methodists think more clearly about their structures and activity in the light of a clear basic ecclesiology and, secondly, to assist mutual understanding between Methodists and those of other Christian traditions. Thirdly, the statement was regarded as a contribution to Christian apologetics. At the turn of the millennium, many of those who are seeking some sort of spirituality find great difficulty in perceiving the churches as attractive or helpful let alone essential to true

Christian living. The Report aimed to show churchly belonging as essential to authentic Christian discipleship. Finally, it was hoped that reflection would aid individuals in ecclesiological reflection. It would help individual Methodists to reassess their own duty and contribution to the Church.[16]

The traditional Methodist emphasis on the Church as essentially missionary was retained but complemented by a stronger trinitarian basis.[17] This accorded both with more recent Methodist emphases on mission as participation in God's mission and with the ecumenical emphasis on trinitarian ecclesiology.[18] The continuity with the Jewish concept of the Covenant people was explored.[19] The traditional Methodist emphasis on the legitimate diversity of church order, as evidenced in the New Testament, was retained and defended in the context of more recent biblical scholarship.[20] The four 'notes' of the church according to the Nicene Creed were expounded.[21] In the third major section entitled 'That the World May Believe', ecumenical experience was given a particularly privileged place. For the first time in a Methodist statement, the distinctively Methodist experience and understanding of the Church were explored in detail. Finally, in the last section, 11 marks of the community that should characterize the Church were identified and offered for reflection.[22]

The central ecclesiological exposition began with a consideration of the trinitarian basis of ecclesiology. Here the preoccupation, in contrast to some other traditions, was less with the relationship of the *koinonia* of the Church to the internal *koinonia* of the persons of the Trinity and more with the total relationship in mission of the triune God to the world.[23] The section begins with the proposition 'If we are to answer fundamental questions about the Church, it is necessary to reflect first on God's relation to the world and his presence in it.' In this way, a distinctively Methodist twist, which takes into account the traditional centrality of mission within Methodism's practical understanding of the Church, is rooted in a wider and ecumenically friendly context. The Church is said to be 'a community called into being by God'. It experiences 'a foretaste of the divine life, intended for all humankind'.[24] It 'derives its very existence and purpose from God's reign and mission, exemplified in and established by Jesus'.[25] The pragmatic and pneumatological basis of much traditional Methodist ecclesiology was reaffirmed in the statement 'the presence of the Holy Spirit alone makes possible the credibility of the Church as a witness and sign in the world of new life in Christ'.[26]

A feature of this trinitarian exposition is the careful balance maintained between emphasizing the fallibility and weakness of the Church and its real nature as a sign pointing to the Kingdom while not yet revealing it in its fullness. The Church was reminded that the mission does not belong to her; rather its vocation is 'to testify to God's reign and to share in his mission'. It is boldly asserted that the New Testament does not know of a perfect Christian community.[27] Nevertheless, we are told that 'the Church is called to mirror [and here there is a direct link made with the nature of the internal *koinonia* of the Trinity], at a finite level, the reality which God is in eternity'. In accordance with the experiential basis of Methodist theology, we are further informed that the missionary nature of the Church as a communion partnership of those equal in God's sight authenticates the Church's understanding of the Trinity as communion.[28]

The emphasis on the Church as sharing in and deriving its nature and function from the trinitarian nature and mission of God was echoed and complemented within the very rich, contemporary insights of the Roman Catholic–Methodist dialogue. In the report *The Apostolic Tradition*, the Church was held to be sustained by a 'conversation initiated by the Lord'. Christ 'gave us His words and waits for us patiently to understand'.[29]

The trinitarian introduction was followed by a consideration of problems that have proved the source of controversy within the relationship of the churches and between Church and synagogue. The concept of the Church as 'covenant people' was stressed both because of the essential relationship of the Church with Judaism and because of the particular Methodist emphasis on 'covenant' and the annual corporate renewal of covenant discipleship in Methodism.[30] The witness of the New Testament both to the concept of the Church as the new covenant people (Heb. 8), as prophesied by Jeremiah, and Paul's witness to God's continuing fidelity to the Jews (Rom. 9–11) was recorded. The Report then comments: 'The biblical witness to God's faithfulness to his people cannot be ignored . . . but Jesus' own prophetic ministry to Israel cannot be set aside either.' The Church must share the gospel with all, including the Jews, in a spirit of dialogue.[31] Thus was a delicate balance maintained. It reflected both the more inclusive and dialogical strands of Universal and particular Methodist tradition as well as the more exclusive ones. In considering the unity and diversity of the Church, as recorded in the New Testament, the Report reinforced the insights of traditional Wesleyan apologetic with the insights of modern biblical scholarship, much of which has been, in turn, deeply influenced by the Methodist scholar James Dunn.[32] Attention was drawn to the 'extraordinary range of images of the Church in the New Testament'. The New Testament itself simultaneously and paradoxically implies that 'diversity – and a sometimes untidy, unharmonious diversity at that – is the norm' while also, through its very unity, precluding the view that 'anything goes'.[33] Three unifying characteristics of the Church's proclamation and activity are identified. They are, first, the determination of the nature and mission of the Church by the paschal mystery and Pentecost. Next comes the common heritage of the Church and Israel. Finally, there is the missionary and doxological expression of the faith. However, 'the diversity of the New Testament precludes a narrow rigidity which attempts to impose a uniform pattern on the Church'.[34] The New Testament may not prescribe an exact pattern of church order or life; it does, however, witness to the interdependence of churches. This interdependence is given a theological basis in the Johannine tradition and a practical application in Paul's appeal for the collection for the Jerusalem church.[35] Finally, an examination of the diversity of Scripture was deemed particularly relevant to the ecumenical era. Methodists needed to attend to what their fellow Christians of other traditions found in Scripture. 'Ecumenical dialogue is thus important since no denomination can do justice, in its faith, life and practice, to the diversity of the NT.' Scripture was itself held to 'warn against a narrow biblicism'.[36] Pragmatic adaptability should accompany enduring faithfulness to the one message and mission of the one Church. Thus was the traditional *sensus fidei* of the Methodist people on ecclesiology upheld and offered for appropriate reception to others.

The consideration of the traditional four credal 'notes' of the Church was grounded in the nature of God's gifts to and requirements of his Church. 'Unity, holiness, catholicity and apostolicity are what God gives to and requires of his Church.' Unity and holiness are particularly identified as 'both gift and aspiration'.[37] The vital nature of unity was strikingly emphasized in the assertion that 'one of the tests of the Church's unity with God is the unity which the Church enjoys within its own life'.[38] The holiness of its members was related both to the unmerited gift of God and to his requirement of human responsibility.[39] Catholicity was related to the generosity of God's love for all creation resulting in a church open to all peoples. It was also related to authenticity of faith which must frequently be the result of a long search and struggle. The traditional Protestantism of Methodism and the modern emphasis upon the 'pilgrim' Church were both reflected in the statement that 'progress' in this was 'neither unilineal nor inevitable'.[40]

Apostolicity was discussed in terms of the 'Lima' consensus on the multifaceted nature of the apostolic tradition, an understanding earlier anticipated in Wesleyan ecclesiology, most notably in the work of Benjamin Gregory.[41] The judgement of the 1937 Statement that the apostolicity of the ministry depended on faithfulness to the totality of the Tradition rather than on a particular form of succession in ministry was cited, though this was balanced both by the statement that succession in ministry can be a valuable sign and by the commitment in the British Methodist Lima Response that 'we await the moment when it would be appropriate to recover the sign of the episcopal succession'.[42] The traditional Methodist refusal to consider the episcopal succession as necessary to authentic churchly existence was balanced by a recognition that the episcopal succession may nevertheless have a 'sign value' in highlighting the apostolic continuity of the Church.

This consideration of the four marks of the Church is followed by a consideration of the necessary characteristics and 'boundaries' of the Church. The centrality of the two gospel sacraments and, particularly, of the Eucharist which 'focuses and expresses both the ongoing and future life of the Church' was stressed. Their celebration was said to be 'normative'. However, this was coupled, in the following paragraph, with a reluctance to 'unchurch' those communities that lacked the sacraments. In a later section of the report, the suggestion was made that though the sacraments are normative and even essential for the whole of the Church, they might not be necessary for every part of it. This suggestion could fruitfully be followed up in wider, multilateral ecumenical dialogue and may be welcome to the Salvation Army and the Society of Friends as taking account of their position.[43]

The interesting assertion was made that though denominations may need to determine their own boundaries, it would be a mistake to define too precisely the boundaries of the Church as a whole.[44] This seemed to reflect the Victorian Wesleyan balance between insistence on the reasonableness of enforcing the discipline of the Connexion within Methodism while accepting, with Gregory, that the Church is 'not a thing of rigid definition'.[45] There was also a hint of a reformed style doctrine of the 'invisible Church'. It was stated in the same paragraph that 'only God knows who are members of the Body of Christ'.[46] This statement could be reconciled with a strand of Wesleyan thinking. Equally, it might be deemed inappropriate in a tradition that defends the prevenient nature of grace shown in the sacrament of Baptism and which clearly believes in God's grace as operative beyond its boundaries.

The final paragraphs stressed the 'indefectibility' of the Church and its eschatological destiny of perfection.[47]

Section 3 of the report dealt with questions of unity and mission which were seen as inherently linked:

> The drive towards the unity of the Church and the renewal
> of the world belong together . . . the more closely Christians
> draw to each other in true *koinonia*, the more fully they will
> be drawn into mission and service in the world.[48]

The wheel has come full circle from the time in the previous
century when Rigg and others had justified denominationalism
as actually enhancing missionary effectiveness.[49] In contrast to
the classical Wesleyan emphasis on the legitimacy of a pattern
of denominations, the phenomenon of denominationalism was
questioned and the strong assertion made that: 'It is unrealistic
to imagine that a unity of this kind [i.e. that implied in an
understanding of *koinonia*] would not be expressed in a visible
and structural union.'[50] It could be argued that this judgement
was both in advance of where many ordinary Methodists are
and yet was re-affirmative of a pattern of official Methodist
ecumenical thinking dating back to the 1930s and reiterated
at the time of the Anglican–Methodist Conversations.[51] The
commitment in *Called to Love and Praise* was in interesting
contrast to the degree of uncertainty within the contemporary
British ecumenical scene. Some then sought closer cooperation
rather than organic unity. Others sought the rather ill-defined
aim of unity in 'reconciled diversity' with its implication, at least
in some quarters, that a degree of denominational autonomy
would continue to exist almost indefinitely. The British
Methodist response to the 'Called to Be One' Process identified
three ways of understanding the concept of 'unity in reconciled
diversity', the weakest of which represented no more than a
continuation of the status quo in ecumenical relationships.[52]
By contrast, *Called to Love and Praise* reiterated a strong
understanding of unity in terms of the 'closest possible
communion, a unity of will, character, purpose, function and
love'.[53] Curiously, in view of the distinctive emphasis of
Methodist connexionalism, mutual accountability was omitted
from this list.

The discussion of the emerging ecumenical emphasis upon
koinonia shows a typical pattern of reception and appropriation

within a Methodist style of understanding. Echoing the Can-
berra statement of 1991, and much earlier ecumenical thought,
koinonia was defined as both 'a gift and a calling', 'a sign and
foretaste of God's intention for humankind'.[54] The Methodist
slant to this reception was shown in the following statement
that 'Koinonia, then, denotes both what Christians share, and
also that sharing is at the heart of the Christian faith ... it is
fundamentally an experience'. The demands of true *koinonia*
are spelt out. 'Co-existence is not enough. Koinonia means a
shared existence. It implies togetherness, mutuality and reci-
procity, requiring mutual recognition and a common acceptance
of each other's identity.'[55]

The continuing problems of ecumenical dialogue were not
ignored. More work was said to be needed, particularly on
church structures, Tradition and the characteristics necessary
for the unity of the Church. The Montreal consensus on tradition was affirmed and related to the so-called Methodist
Quadrilateral. 'Methodists can welcome the recent ecumenical
emphasis on tradition as dynamic, rather than static, as a shared,
"lived experience" rather than simply a deposit of doctrine.'[56]
Once again, this Methodist reception harks back to Wesley's
evaluation and estimation of the life of the Primitive Church
and the reaffirmation of this by Quick and others.[57] A final
paragraph indicated that the Methodist commitment to ecumenism and understanding and reception of the ecclesiology of
koinonia would be put to the test in the imminent sets of unity
conversations in all three countries within Britain.[58]

The second part of section 3, devoted to mission, was carefully nuanced to take account both of the traditional Methodist
emphasis on evangelism and of more modern emphases on social
justice and service. It also took account of the immense change
in mainstream Christian attitudes towards other faiths. The
theological underpinning of its very sensitive approach came
from an understanding of the nature of God. Thus authentically
Christian evangelism would be 'vulnerable, patient and loving'.[59]
Since the gospel had to be 'both spoken and lived' there was a
necessary dual commitment to evangelism and to peace and

justice, though it was legitimate for individual Christians to vary their personal emphases within this dual commitment.[60]

It was clearly emphasized that the correct Christian approach to people of other faiths could not be determined simply by appealing to particular texts in Scripture. Scripture itself revealed a variety of approaches, some exclusive, some more inclusive; they ought always to be interpreted contextually. Christians might gladly affirm all that was true and holy in other religions. The task of sharing in God's mission to those of other religions necessarily involved dialogue, defined as 'not only sharing the Christian faith, but listening to the understanding others have of God, life and salvation' and 'working with them for peace and justice'.[61] Caution was needed in sharing in acts of worship with those of other faiths in order not to compromise one's own beliefs; nevertheless, attendance at such worship could be a vital learning experience.[62] Appeal was made to Wesley's own occasional affirmation of the genuine holiness of some adherents of other religions.[63]

The ambiguity of the process of 'inculturation' was also affirmed. The gospel had to be translated into the terms of each culture to which it came; nevertheless all cultures, including those influenced by Christianity, continued to need transformation by the gospel. The conclusion to the section was, perhaps, necessarily ambiguous. Christians were at the beginning of a process of dialogue, the outcome of which was unpredictable.

> Christians may enter such dialogues in the faith that God will give them deeper insight into the truth of Christ. People of other faiths can hardly be said to belong to the Church. But the Church has to be understood in a way which does not deny the signs of God in their midst.[64]

The implication, surely not new, was that the Church was not the exclusive sphere of God's action. God might, at least in part, reveal himself beyond its boundaries.

The long section on Methodism had a dual purpose. The first was the ecumenical one of explaining Methodism to other churches and offering insights from the Methodist experience of being church, 'as part of Methodism's distinctive contribution to the wider Church'. The second was to enable Methodists to understand their own ecclesiological development and to aid a necessary process of discernment:

> in order to distinguish between those features of Methodist history and tradition which should be cherished and handed on to the wider Church and those which need to be abandoned, or adapted, because they no longer contribute creatively to contemporary Christian life.[65]

This second declared purpose represented a challenge to Methodists to display maturity in deciding which aspects of their tradition were abiding contributions to the Great Tradition of the Church and which were merely ephemeral without abiding relevance.

This 'Methodist' section of *Called to Love and Praise* has been criticized for not saying enough about Methodist worship, a criticism that seems unfounded in view of the fact that there is a clear statement of certain key balances within the Methodist worshipping tradition, most notably the balance between the more formal 'liturgical' style, inherited originally from Anglicanism, and the emphasis on the more lyrical celebratory nature of Methodist worship, as well as upon the more informal and extempore elements in it.[66] The main report was completed just a little early to comment on the rapid changes in the style of hymnody used within parts of Methodism. Until the early 1980s the use of a standard hymn book was as characteristic of Methodism as, somewhat earlier, had been the use of the *Book of Common Prayer* in mainstream Anglicanism. The last twenty years have seen the end, for better or worse, of that monopoly and the widespread adoption, albeit usually alongside some continuing use of the 'official' hymn book, of alternative, mostly contemporary, forms of hymnody already in widespread use elsewhere. The use of such 'worship song books' as *Songs of Fellowship* and *Mission Praise* is particularly widespread. *Called to Love and Praise* also just predated the new *Methodist Worship Book* of 1999, with its unprecedentedly rich resources for 'liturgical' worship. The exact effect of the new book on the balance and ethos of British Methodist worship remains to be seen.

Perhaps a more substantial criticism of the report would be to say that it almost entirely failed to deal with the nature of internal Methodist diversity and how it is handled and assessed today. No substantial reference was made to the Methodist divisions of the nineteenth century and their legacy in popular piety and attitudes. Nor was there any real consideration of the diversities that have arisen from the influence of purely twentieth-century movements. Both the charismatic and liturgical movements have influenced many contemporary Methodists. Probably modern Methodism embraces a wider diversity of styles of worship, devotion and theological approach than in any previous era. On occasion, within modern times, these have threatened division. Had the Anglican–Methodist Conversations of the 1960s succeeded, they might well have resulted in some withdrawing from Methodism to create a 'continuing Methodist' Church not in communion with the Church of England. The controversy over sexuality in the early nineties could also have led to schism, at least on a small scale, had the issue not been so delicately handled. Not long ago, a recently retired Chairman of District told me that it was no longer possible, as it had been in his youth, to send any minister anywhere in the Connexion. There were now churches that would refuse to accept the ministry of certain ministers whose theological stance they could not accept.[67] Where does that leave the 'connexionalism' practised historically in Methodism and still celebrated in the report?[68]

Some consideration of these questions could, perhaps, have figured in the main historical section, 'From Society to Church'. As written, this section was nevertheless a valuable resource for understanding many of the characteristics of Methodism.[69] It contained one error, the suggestion that the class meeting disappeared except for its revival in the university situation. In fact, quite a few churches have retained class meetings, even if they meet less frequently than the classical weekly norm. Their present purpose is for small-group fellowship and education, not the close discipline and spiritual oversight of yesteryear. However, Methodists of the eighteenth and nineteenth centuries would still be able to identify with their pastoral function and their value in terms of mutual support.[70]

Two sub-sections confronted issues especially important within twentieth-century Methodism. First, the question of 'membership' was dealt with in sub-section 4.4, 'The Relationship of the Individual to the Church Community in Methodism'. Next came the relationship between the doctrine of the priesthood of all believers and the doctrine of the ministry, in subsection 4.5.

In late twentieth-century Methodism, the understanding of the relationship between baptism (and more recently also 'confirmation') and membership has changed considerably. Whilst infant baptism was always regarded as significant and valid, being stoutly and regularly defended within the last generation or so against some who would like to see Methodism move to a 'believers' baptist position, it was, perhaps, popularly regarded very much more as a declaratory act of God's prevenient grace and an act of adoption into the nurturing body of the Church rather than as the sacrament that conferred full membership of the Church.[71]

By contrast, 'reception into membership' was regarded as the key point at which a person entered into the responsible exercise of Christian membership. In 1894, a service of 'reception into membership' had been devised in order to emphasize that this was responsible membership of the Church Universal and not just a societary membership.[72] The 1975 *Service Book* included a joint service of confirmation/reception into membership which, for the first time, included a rite of the laying on of hands in the Anglican confirmation tradition.[73] This raised the question of what happened when a person, to use traditional Methodist terminology, 'ceased to meet', in the sense of failing to attend worship and relinquishing all real contact with the local church.

Certainly such people had never been regarded as forfeiting their baptismal membership in the Universal Church. It was now also felt that they were not forfeiting their confirmation. Clearly, work is needed on this. It needs to address the question of relating the inherited societal concept of 'membership' to the understanding of baptism and confirmation. It must also take account of the complex ecumenical debate simultaneously taking place on the theology of initiation.[74]

The sub-section also reaffirmed the traditional Methodist understanding of baptism as being 'of divine appointment and perpetual obligation' and its significance as a witness to the primacy of God's grace and the role of the Church as nurturing institution.[75] The importance of the baptized individual later making an explicit commitment to the responsible exercise of their membership of the Church was stressed in the words 'individual Christian decision remains important'.[76] Active responsible membership through a local church was emphasized as a norm of Christian discipleship.

> An individual's commitment to Christ can truly be realised only in full participation in the worship, witness and service of the Christian community and this is normally best achieved through the local church and the web of its relationships with others.

Regular attendance as an 'adherent', a long-term practice among some linked with Methodism, was labelled 'something of an anomaly'.[77] The section concluded with the assertion that the loss of a sense of responsibility for the local church would be a great loss.[78]

The question of membership has become entangled with the financial arrangements of Methodism and with attempts in many cases to remove inactive persons from membership in order to 'reduce the assessment'. A recent draft report to the Conference suggested a new approach to the counting of membership and of the financial responsibilities of local churches to the wider Connexion. The whole matter proved controversial and the original was thrown back for further consideration. The question will continue to engage Methodism for the foreseeable future.[79] It may be that this particular sub-section of the report will become dated much more rapidly than most others, even though it did raise some fundamental issues.

The other question was that of the relationship of the doctrine of the priesthood of all believers to the doctrine of the ministry.[80] For many Methodists in the more radical non-Wesleyan traditions, the doctrine of the priesthood of all believers was seen as justifying an understanding of ordained ministry that left it as purely functional and clearly subordinate to the wishes of the lay majority both within the Connexion and within the local church situation. Before Methodist reunion, lay presidency at the Eucharist had also been common within the non-Wesleyan churches, particularly within the ex-Free Methodist section of the United Methodist Church.[81] Many Methodists continue to believe that lay presidency should be allowed more or less as a matter of course, rather than being, as is the case in modern British Methodism, confined to very particular and narrowly defined situations of proven eucharistic deprivation.[82] Though the Wesleyan Church had never allowed lay presidency, it had always strongly upheld the doctrine of the priesthood of all believers. However, it had never seen it as legitimizing the view that 'anyone could do anything' within the Church. Rather, the Wesleyan emphasis was primarily a protest against the idea that grace was exclusively dependent on the sacramental ministrations of episcopally ordained presbyters and that grace was not also present in the non-sacramental means of grace.[83]

Section 4.5 emphasized that the sole individual and primary priesthood in the New Testament is that of Christ.[84] It then asserted that the New Testament 'directs us to the priesthood of the body of believers, rather than the priesthood of every believer', but it failed to make the point that even that corporate priesthood is strictly derivative by participation from that of Christ (though this could be implicitly derived from the discussion of the Reformers' understanding of baptism in para. 4.5.6).[85] It offered a sop to the more individualistic understanding of the priesthood of all believers in saying that the 'latter emphasis is not necessarily wrong'.[86] The way in which the New Testament applied cultic language to Christian daily life rather than to any act of worship was emphasized. This allowed the section to move on to the traditional Methodist emphasis on the 'ministry of the whole people of God', as an aspect of the royal priesthood of the faithful. The emphasis on the total corporate ministry of the whole Church had been recently reasserted in the 1990 Conference report, *The Ministry of the People of God*.[87] This ministry was accordingly seen as 'the primary and normative ministry of the Church'.[88]

From here the discussion moved on to a discussion of the distinctive ministry of presbyters.[89] The traditional emphasis enshrined within the Deed of Union that 'ordination does not confer any special priestly powers on the minister' was reasserted.[90] However, alongside this, a high doctrine of the presbyterate was enunciated, arguably going beyond the merely functional. The teaching of the 1974 'Statement on Ordination' was reaffirmed alongside its nature as a ministry of enablement, 'leading the people to share with them in their calling'. This was followed by the statement: 'In this sense they are the sign of the presence and ministry of Christ in the Church, and through the Church to the world.'[91]

The concern of the Statement to locate presbyteral ministry, indeed all ministries, firmly within the context of the whole people of God cohered with the modern ecumenical consensus. That consensus is upheld even by those churches which do argue that the ordained presbyter participates in a unique way in the priesthood of Christ, even though that participation is orientated to the service of the royal priesthood of all the faithful.[92] Further work needs to be done ecumenically within all the major traditions on this question.

The 1937 Statement had emphasized the dual origin of ordained ministry as something that both arose within the Church and was discerned and authorized by it, yet was also God's gift to the Church.[93] In using the language of 'sign' the Report, whatever the exact intentions of the working party and the understanding of those who approved the Report in the 1999 Conference, was using quasi-sacramental language. It did not go all the way with the language of 'iconic' representation that characterizes some present-day Roman Catholic and Orthodox theology of ministerial priesthood, but it left the door open to an affirmation of the real ontological importance of the presbyterate, understood, however, always in the context of the prior corporate priesthood of the people of God.[94] The function of the presbyterate was to act as a constant sign and reminder of the wider *koinonia* of the Church within the local church and circuit. That underlay the emphasis in para. 8 on the fact that eucharistic presidency is normally confined to presbyters, as representative of the wider Church (and even when not so confined is always authorized on behalf of the whole Connexion) as a reminder that 'the Eucharist is not a private, or even simply a local matter'. Presbyters in Methodism are ordained at the Conference, rather than in local churches as is the custom in some other traditions. This is to express their status as servants of the whole Church and not simply of a local church or churches.[95]

This brings us to the way in which connexionalism was expounded both within the specific section devoted to it and elsewhere in the Report.[96] As we have already seen in earlier chapters, connexionalism had previously been regarded as a Methodist 'peculiar institution'. It had been vigorously defended by the nineteenth-century Wesleyans as an entirely proper and efficient way of organizing a church orientated to mission.[97] Implicitly, the great Wesleyan ecclesiologists had regarded it as superior to other forms of church organization while never actually commending its adoption by other churches. In the early twentieth century, all branches of reunited Methodism had taken it for granted that some form of connexionalism would prevail within the reunited Church, though there were varying views about the degree of authority that should be given both to the presbyterate and to local churches within a connexional framework.[98] In the early and middle years of the century, it continued to be taken for granted that connexionalism was a

Methodist peculiar institution. In the more irenic ecumenical atmosphere of the time, there was no desire to push its claims upon others.

By the early 1990s, as a result both of internal pressures and ecumenical developments, the time was ripe for a renewed examination of connexionalism. Both the steep decline in membership from the 1960s and the administrative restructuring of Methodism in the 1970s led to more questioning of connexionalism. Methodist involvement in Local Ecumenical Partnerships had led to a degree of interest in connexionalism on the part of ecumenical partners, some of whom warmly applauded the sense of wide community within Methodism to which the connexional spirit testified. In 1991, Brian Beck, the Secretary of the Conference, produced a brace of brilliant articles on the subject.[99] A leading Roman Catholic ecumenist, George Tavard, who had a particularly deep knowledge of Methodism arising from his participation in the international Catholic–Methodist dialogue and also from teaching in an American Methodist university, called for dialogue on connexionalism.[100]

True to Methodist tradition, the Report endorsed connexionalism both theologically and pragmatically. It was held to 'enshrine a vital truth about the nature of the Church', witnessing to 'a mutuality and interdependence which derive from the participation of all Christians through Christ in the very life of God himself'.[101] It was also asserted that individual churches do not function effectively in isolation and that connexionalism helps point up necessary priorities in mission and service.[102] For the first time in Methodist history, Methodism 'commends this principle to other churches'.[103] This commendation was balanced, first, by the admission that the connexional principle had not always 'come to expression in a complete or balanced way in Methodist structures', and secondly by pointing to the way in which the connexionalism was, or could be, compatible with other patterns of ministry. Since connexionalism involved the recognition of the need for ministries of oversight, traditionally largely exercised corporately within British Methodism, it was open to the exploration of the personally focused ministries of bishops and of the 'Petrine office'.[104] It had already been held, in the context of the 'covenanting' discussions of the late 1970s, that the adoption of episcopacy would not violate Methodist doctrinal standards.[105] It was also noted, in one of the few references to the practice of another sister Methodist church in the Report, that, in American Methodism, bishops and conferences shared in the work of oversight.[106] Finally, a reference to the ultimate possibility of a Methodist reception of a universal primacy as essential to the unity of the Church, first adumbrated in the context of ecclesiological debate within the Roman Catholic–Methodist international dialogue, was made.[107]

These statements represented important ecumenical openings. Already, the Conference has approved a statement on episkope and episcopacy which in 2000 it commended for study. It aims at offering guidance to Methodist representatives in negotiations with 'episcopal' churches.[108] Methodist exploration of the Petrine ministry has also begun in a small way.[109] For many other reasons, quite apart from the matter of reaching agreement on an acceptable understanding of the Petrine ministry in working practice, it is unlikely there will be any substantial advance on this for many years. The combination of careful theological evaluation of connexionalism and ecumenical openness to new possibilities of reconciling connexionalism with other ecclesiologies reveals a degree of welcome ecclesiological and ecumenical maturity.

Stress was laid on the fact that connexionalism 'naturally precludes both independency and autocracy as models of church government'.[110] The former point did not militate against a very real concern for the principle of subsidiarity and the concession of the maximum possible freedom to local churches, circuits and districts to make the decisions that fit their particular situations.[111] It should reassure those traditions that emphasize the proper autonomy of the local church that entering into union with a connexional church would not mean the end of all reasonable local autonomy. Neither, however, does it exclude the possibility that personally focused ministries of oversight might come to play a greater role within Methodism in the future. The

Methodist concern remains for partnership at every level. Such partnership always involves mutual listening and common decision making while respecting the very special role of the presbyterate, which, in any case, as section 4.5 insists, is constituted by the commissioning of the whole. In an era in which the ecclesiology of *koinonia*/communion is predominant in ecumenical ecclesiology, Methodism can commend connexionalism as an authentic Methodist *typos* and reception of *koinonia*. One omission in the report is perhaps noteworthy – the failure to explore explicitly the witness of the internationally organized United Methodist Church of the USA to the logic of a global connexionalism.[112] Consideration of the Petrine ministry, however tentative, also points in the direction of a global connexionalism, albeit through a personally focused ministry rather than corporate oversight by a global General Conference. The developing closer links with European Methodist churches, many of them in connexion with the United Methodist Church, may also point towards a future global connexionalism. The concluding section, 4.7, asserts that 'at this international level, the connexional principle propels Methodist churches towards a sharing of resources which crosses both denominational and national boundaries'.[113] The penultimate reference points to the fact that connexionalism has a necessarily ecumenical orientation in terms of a necessary relationship with all churches that we recognize as sister churches.

The section on connexionalism naturally led on to a brief review of current Methodist structures, designed to raise questions about their conformity to the ideal and practice of true connexionalism. Cautions were given against the tendency for some bigger local churches to adopt a practically independent and self-sufficient line and about the failure of those with connexional responsibilities to foster the mutual understanding between local and connexional levels that the system necessitates.[114] Finally, Methodists were exhorted to be pragmatic and flexible in their approach to terminology and to change. They should be prepared to defend the essential principle of inter-relatedness, while yielding on particular details.[115]

In conclusion, one may say that *Called to Love and Praise* is an admirably constructive document, simultaneously loyal to the heart of the Methodist tradition as it has evolved over the last couple of centuries and open to the insights of modern scholarship and ecumenism. It ends with a vision of what the Church should be in practical Christian community living. It couples this with an expression of the hope that, should Methodism cease to exist as a separate entity within the twenty-first century, it would, nevertheless, be able to contribute some of the riches of its own distinctive history to any future united Church. Considerable interest has been shown by our American sister church in *Called to Love and Praise* and it is to be hoped that some of its insights will enter into the life stream of world Methodism and the yet wider Church beyond.[116]

5

The Methodist Doctrine of Ministry

Much has already been said about the evolution of the practice and doctrine of the ordained ministry in Methodism. It is impossible to study ecclesiology in any tradition without reference to its concept of ministry. The purpose of this chapter is threefold. First, it is to attempt some assessment of enduring emphases within Methodist theology and practice. Secondly, we shall consider the implications of the statements on ordination of 1960 and 1974 and later developments in diaconal ministry and in the discussion of episcopacy and the nature of the 'ministry of the people of God'. Finally, we shall consider the Methodist contribution to ecumenical thinking about ordained ministry.

There would appear to be three enduring characteristics of Methodist thinking about the ordained ministry from the time of Wesley onwards. The first is the emphasis upon the basically pastoral nature of ministry. The prime concern of the Wesleys was that there should be a ministry that trained souls in holiness and watched over them in love. It was to secure this for his people that Wesley conferred pastoral functions upon the travelling preachers even though he insisted that they were not ministers of sacrament as well as word. The emphasis upon the basically pastoral nature of ordained ministry continued across all the vicissitudes of the nineteenth century. The claim that ordained ministers had exclusive pastoral prerogatives was gradually dropped and the acceptance of the co-pastoral leadership of others was asserted in the Deed of Union. Nevertheless, ordained ministers continued to be seen as having special responsibility for pastoral care and oversight. Methodism continued to emphasize that it exercised effective episkope in which ministers had a special role. The Roman Catholic–Methodist dialogue of recent times has mentioned the pastoral nature of ministry as a key emphasis in both traditions.[1]

Secondly, Methodists have emphasised ministry as located securely within the Church, not above it (as in traditional Anglo- and Roman Catholic thought) or below it, as in churches of 'independent' ecclesiology. The ministry certainly arises within the Church and is responsible to it, but it is also seen as God's gift to the Church.[2] Even in the days of Buntingite emphasis upon the prerogatives of the Pastoral Office, acknowledgement was made of the former. Thus, we read Bunting writing in 1850 of 'men especially called of God, and then especially set apart by the **concurrence** of the Church – the ministry and the people together – to take charge, as its pastors, of the purity of the body'.[3] The 'concurrence' of the Church was duly acknowledged along with the call of God which the Church had to discern and act upon.

Finally, there is the Methodist emphasis upon the variability and adaptability of ministry. That there should be the 'pastoral office' within the Church with its divinely allotted functions of teaching and oversight was regarded as an indisputable, scriptural principle. That it should take the form of the threefold ministry as it emerged from the second century onwards, or that it should always be transmitted through unbroken episcopal succession, was not regarded as scripturally proven or provable. To Methodists, the precise ordering of the Church and ministry was seen as a matter of sensible adaptation to changing exigencies. Methodists were and are concerned that essential functions be carried out rather than that they always be carried out in the same manner. They were prepared to identify parallels between the way Methodism had developed and the way the early Church had done. Many Wesleyans argued that the institution of the diaconate had been the first example of apostolic improvisation; Methodism in its institution of stewards had replicated the apostolic principle of creating an auxiliary ministry.[4] The beauty of the Methodist insight was and is its adaptability to changing situations. As recent thinking about episkope and episcopacy has shown, Methodists are able simultaneously to affirm the reality of non-episcopal ministries and churches, while recognizing the legitimacy of an episcopally structured church and even showing preparedness to receive the 'gift of the episcopal succession' in the context of furthering the unity of Christ's Church.[5]

Methodism, lacking absolute commitment to specific 'divine right' theories of ministry, is nevertheless able to respond to and receive the insights of others as they tend towards the fuller building up of the Body of Christ.[6]

The years 1960 to 1990 saw British Methodism remain loyal to the perennial insights outlined above while reacting creatively both to ecumenical challenges and opportunities and to new internal developments. Much changed in the Methodist practice of ordained ministry. Provision was made for ministers of other churches with which Methodism cooperated in a growing number of Local Ecumenical Projects (now called local ecumenical partnerships) to be 'recognized and regarded' or 'authorized' ministers. The former category of ministers were to enjoy, during the period concerned, all the privileges of a Methodist minister and to be subject, where their work with Methodists was concerned, to full Methodist discipline. The latter were authorized to give pastoral care to Methodists though not being fully regarded, pro tem, as Methodist ministers.

After debates reaching back into the thirties, and after a delay while Methodism awaited the outcome of the proposals for unity with the Church of England, the decision was finally taken to admit women to presbyteral ministry. This decision, in 1974, brought British Methodism into line with the practice of many other Methodist churches around the world. It occasioned no serious theologically based opposition, though some were concerned about the practical problems of 'stationing' women ministers under the constraint either of looking after children or fitting in with the location of a partner's work. After the admission of women to presbyteral ministry, the question arose of the future of the deaconess order, the one form of ordained ministry previously open to women. Many deaconesses now entered the presbyteral ministry. Recruitment for the Wesley Deaconess Order dropped and it was closed. However, in 1988, the Order was reopened as the Diaconal Order, open now to both men and women. Some time was spent in rethinking the theology of the newly widened diaconate. Though deaconesses had been ordained by prayer and the laying on of hands, they had always been classed for constitutional purposes as layfolk. There was a clear tension between what *The Constitutional Practice and Discipline of the Methodist Church* said and what the ordination services implied. Accordingly, the Deed of Union, which recognized only one order of ministers, was revised in 1993 to allow for the recognition of the ministerial status of deacons.

A further development was that of 'sector' and 'locally ordained' ministries. Until the 1960s, all Methodist ministers were still subject to the traditional discipline of itinerancy. Only a few were not in circuit appointments. Of these, some were in 'connexional' jobs, for example, officers of the connexional departments. Yet others were 'permitted to serve' with external organizations, many of them as academics in colleges or universities. Permission to serve was far from easily granted. From the sixties, an increasing number of ministers felt that they should serve with other organizations, and believed that, in so doing, they were still acting as 'representative' persons, signalling the Church's presence. Some other churches began to develop forms of non-stipendiary and purely local ordained ministry. Methodism began to realize that such expedients might offer the chance of attracting into presbyteral ministry people of maturity and calibre who, for various reasons, could not easily offer for traditional itinerant ministry.

In due course, provision was made both for 'sector' ministers, including an arrangement for people to candidate as such while remaining in their 'secular' employment, and for 'ministers in local appointment', who might or might not also have a secular job, but who would remain in their home circuit and serve there.[7] At the same time, the development of new lay ministries, such as those of 'lay pastoral workers', and a renewed emphasis upon the ministry of the whole people of God, provided yet another context for the reassessment of ministry, lay as well as ordained. Meanwhile, increased ecumenical cooperation at the local level, combined with the 'Covenanting' scheme of the seventies plus the later revival of talks with the Church of England from 1994, meant that the ecumenical dimension was never far from Methodist minds.[8]

Resulting from these influences and new provisions came a series of important statements which represented, cumulatively, a very significant development and enrichment of Methodist thinking about ministry. In them loyalty to traditional Methodist emphases was combined with positive and flexible responses to new thinking both within Methodism and the wider Church. We shall consider in turn the statements on ordination of 1960 and 1974, the investigation of episcopacy between 1978 and 1982, the theology of the newly restructured diaconate and the statements on the ministry of the whole people of God.[9]

The statements on ordination responded both to ecumenical and internal exigencies. The 1960 statement was regarded by its proponents as a gloss on the thinking of the 1937 ecclesiological statement, *Nature of the Christian Church*. It quotes its statement that,

> In the New Testament, the ministry of the Word and Sacraments is a divine gift to the Church . . . it was a ministry within the Church, exercising in the name and by the authority of the Lord, who is Head of the Church, power and functions which are inherent in the Church.

It further emphasized that, 'a minister is Christ's ambassador and the representative of the whole people of God'.[10] Ministry was to be seen thus neither as solely representative of the people nor as solely representative of God, thus avoiding both hierarchicalism and independency and clearly locating the ministry within the Church and its total ministry, lay and ordained. In pursuit of this it was stressed that no one had an 'absolute' right to ordain others within Methodism; ordinations were always

carried out on the authority of the Conference.[11] The claim of
the ordained ministry of Methodism to authenticity both on
scriptural grounds and those of later tradition was clearly stated.
'The Methodist Church believes that its ministry is ordered in
harmony with the teaching of the New Testament. There is a
single ministry equivalent to that of the "presbyter-bishops" in
the New Testament.' Thus, the claim of Methodism to have a
ministry that performed the essential functions of the emerging
ministry of the apostolic and sub-apostolic ages was put forward.[12] Such an assertion, however, did not prevent Methodism
from later considering positively the possible reception of a
separate episcopal ministry within the 'historic succession'.
Methodism respected the principle of adaptability as one that
could involve reception from others.

The 1974 statement further developed the concept of the
minister as 'representative' person within the context of the
renewed emphasis upon the ministry of the whole people of
God in the Church. 'Ordination can be seen afresh in a situation
where it is the entire laos [i.e. people] of God who share in the
ministry of Christ.'[13] There was a desire to transcend sterile
ecumenical debates as to the priority of the 'ontological' or the
'functional' in presbyteral ministry. Implicitly, the 1974 statement argues that a presbyteral minister must both have a function and be a sign. What he or she receives is a special calling
within a general calling. 'In this sense, they are the sign of the
presence and ministry of Christ in the Church, and through the
Church to the world.'[14] Such an understanding is, of course,
linked to the 'sign' concept of the Church as 'sign, instrument
and first fruits' of the Kingdom.

In the ecumenical context this modern British Methodist
emphasis can be seen as providential, opening the way for a
common ecumenical consensus that transcends the old polarities
of 'functional' and 'ontological' concepts of the ministry. A key
remaining challenge for Methodists is to reformulate their
understanding of the minister as 'representative person' in the
light of recent advances in the understanding of the Church as
koinonia and of ministry in other traditions, as essentially service

of *koinonia*. Such a reformulation would accord with Benjamin Gregory's understanding of the presbyterate.[15]

Both reports gave some attention to the continuing link between 'reception into full connexion' and ordination. The 1974 report was not entirely clear on the matter. It first said that neither ceremony was really complete without the other, but then went on to add that now that they were separated, it was clear that it was ordination that actually conveyed authority.[16] This can be seen as an implicit recognition that it is in carrying out the universally recognized sign of ordination by prayer and the laying on of hands, rather than by the purely Methodist ceremony of 'reception into full connexion', that Methodists can claim that theirs is a true ministry of word and sacraments within the Universal Church and not simply within Methodism.

The 'representative person' doctrine of the ministry coheres well with recent thought on the apostolicity of the Church which stresses that the whole Church is apostolic, while needing a special ministry of oversight to help guard its apostolicity. Such thinking also sees continuity in ministry as a valuable sign of apostolicity, though not necessarily a guarantee of it.[17] One can argue that the doctrine is illuminated by the specifically Methodist practice of itinerancy. Traditionally, Methodist ministers itinerated not only in the interests of evangelistic coverage of the nation but also in the interests of maintaining *koinonia* and the cohesion of the Connexion. The practice visibly illustrated to the grass-roots Methodist the connexional nature of the Church. Ministers were guardians of orthodoxy, appointed to watch over each other and their flocks. The Methodist people knew that those stationed among them by the authority of the Conference had to answer searching questions as to their loyalty to the Methodist doctrine and discipline. They represented the faith of the whole church to the local church which, in its turn, could discern in them that faith which they had received from their predecessors.[18] In a similar manner, as the research of Jean-Marie Tillard has shown, early Christian communities chose as bishops those in whom they could see the apostolic

faith reflected. They then had confidence that they would maintain that faith and represent it in the koinonia of the wider
Church.[19] Methodist presbyters still represent the teaching of
the Universal Church to their people, and the sensus fidelium,
the common spiritual instinct of the faithful, recognizes in them
faithfulness to the Tradition. Methodist understanding of this
function thus coheres well with the emerging ecumenical consensus that ministry is above all the servant of koinonia.

Towards the end, the 1974 statement picked up the question
of the diaconate. Its conclusions on the matter were, understand-
ably, somewhat tentative in view both of the Methodist understanding of diaconal ministry and the complex heritage of
diaconal ministry in the rest of Christendom. It was immediately
stated that 'the differentia of the diaconal ministry is less easy
to define than that of the presbyterate. To render service is the
duty of every . . . Christian.' The statement immediately went
on to identify a tension within Methodist theology and practice.

In Methodism we ordain deaconesses but we do not have
deacons, for we have said, the Reformation office of 'deacon',
clearly corresponding to the NT 'diaconos' is held amongst
us by the various kinds of 'stewards' who are called to per-
form their stewardship to the glory of God and the building
up of the Church.

Methodism had, in fact, been operating with two concepts of
the diaconate. One focused on the servant ministry of women
who, by candidating successfully for it, thereby also became
members of a religious order and accepted a discipline of availability similar to that of presbyters in Methodism. The other
made an informal, and not necessarily correct, identification of
a specifically Methodist set of ministries with the diaconate of
the New Testament and the Reformation.[20]

Various possibilities for the future were canvassed. They
included abandoning the concept of the diaconate as an order
of ministry and seeing it purely as a religious order. As the
report noted, however, the position of the presently ordained

members of the Wesley Deaconess Order had to be taken into account.[21]

Methodism was to act ahead of any full resolution of the theological problems involved. In 1988, the Conference resolved that deacons and deaconesses be ordained as deacons in the 'Church of God' and instructed the Faith and Order Committee to study and report upon the theological and constitutional problems to be addressed.[22] Methodism had created and had provided liturgically for a second order of ministry. How was this now to be understood? Further reports in the 1990s addressed the issue, concluding, in the spirit of Methodist thinking about the 'representative' nature of ministry, that:

> Deacons and deaconesses are a focus for the servant ministry of Christ; through their ministry of caring, the incarnate servant Christ is revealed. They are a 'focus' for the servant ministry of the Church, making visible God's calling to the Church to be a servant in the world. Their servant ministry challenges the Church to respond to this calling . . . Diaconal ministry particularly focuses the servant ministry of Christ just as presbyteral ministry focuses the priestly and prophetic ministry of Christ and the Church.[23]

The last sentence quoted encapsulates the difference between diaconal and presbyteral ministry. It was accompanied, however, by the statement that all specific ministries are rooted 'first in the total ministry of Christ Himself and secondly in the ministry of the people of God'. The servant nature of lay and presbyteral ministry was not denied by the existence of the focusing ministry of deacons. Finally, it was asserted that the Diaconal Order was both an order of ministry and a religious order.

Had the 'Covenanting' proposals of the late 1970s come to fruition, Methodism would have found itself adopting a third form of ordained ministry, the episcopal. Much work was done on episcopacy between 1978 and 1982, the key question being how a personally focused episcopal ministry would relate to the Conference as the traditional corporate instrument of episkope

in Methodism.[24] The stance taken towards episcopacy was positive, but loyal to previous Methodist tradition. The 1981 statement began with the assertion:

> The Conference believes that the coming great church will be
> congregational, presbyteral and episcopal in its life and order.
> One step towards this would be for the Methodist church to
> include an episcopal form of ministry in its life. This would
> be a sign of faith in the future and a way of helping churches
> with and without bishops in the search for unity.[25]

The report even went so far as to suggest that, should other
churches delay in responding to the process, Methodism might
even consider taking the step of adopting episcopacy separately.[26] Such assertions and such a proposal indicated the strong
Methodist commitment to Christian unity. As we shall see in
the final chapter, the approach taken at the dawn of the eighties
was bolder and more positive than it was to be when Methodism
reconsidered the question at the turn of the millennium. The
report showed a real attempt to grapple with the witness of the
majority in Christendom to the value of the episcopal succession.
'While we ask, "Why bishops?", the majority of our fellow
Christians ask, "Why not bishops?"' The Methodist principle
of necessary adaptability to new conditions was being implicitly
invoked. The fact that episcopacy could not be definitely proved
to be scripturally required was no reason for rejecting it.
Methodists had accepted it in the Indian unity schemes. Provided
Methodists were not, by adopting the historic episcopate, committed to denying their previous churchly status, 'a step that
helps unity and mission, while not denying God's grace in any
way, is in keeping with Scripture and our Methodist tradition'.[27]

The report stated: 'The important issue touches not on the
fact of the historic episcopate but the way it is exercised and
the way it is received.'[28] A Methodist episcopate would have to
be related in its oversight to other ministers and to lay people.
It was stated that: 'Our view of a bishop includes some of the
characteristics or tasks traditionally associated with bishops (a

focus of unity and continuity, a guardian of doctrine, an ordainer). Some of these, however, would be differently expressed in our tradition.' Methodist episcopacy would be fundamentally missionary and pastoral (relating, one might add, parenthetically, to the traditional missionary and pastoral nature of the presbyterate among Methodists). The stress on the brotherhood of the ministry would mean that presbyters would be seen as the bishop's colleagues rather than subordinates. The place of Synod and Conference would mean that the bishops would never take decisions in isolation. The bishops' representative leadership would mean that they would represent the concerns of their areas to the Conference and the wider Church and would, in turn, represent the concerns of the latter to their people. Episcopal ministry would represent 'genuine partnership' with others.[29]

In all of this, the 1981 report paralleled, or even anticipated, much of the developing thinking within the Anglican and Roman Catholic churches on episcopal ministry. In both of these traditions, increasing emphasis was falling on the collaborative and collegial nature of episcopal ministry. Roman Catholics stressed the collegial collaboration and responsibility of bishops. Anglicans emphasized the collaboration of bishops with other clergy and lay people.[30]

Considerable thought was given as to which sorts of ministers might be made bishops. Should it be Presidents of the Conference, or Chairs of Districts or superintendent ministers?[31] In many ways, the last-named exercise the most purely personal, supervisory ministry within Methodism. The question remained an academic one when the Covenant failed. Methodism subsequently had little stomach for the possibility of adopting episcopacy separately.

Finally came the reports on the 'Ministry of the People of God', summing up the long Methodist tradition, affirmed in all branches of Methodism before the union of 1932, that Methodism both needed and valued the various ministries of lay people, whether informal, or formally constituted and recognized in the Constitutional Practice and Discipline of the

Methodist Church.[32] The two reports, issued in 1986 and 1988, worked from the fundamental insight enshrined in the 1974 Statement on Ordination, that presbyteral ministry focused the 'calling of the whole Church'. What, then did 'the calling of the whole Church' mean for those both in ordained ministry and those not? The 1986 report stated:

> The Spirit sanctifies us (1 Cor. 6:11, 1 Thess. 5:23), makes us God's saints, sets apart for God's service (Rom. 1:7, 1 Cor. 1:2). Our service, or ministry, is the life of love for God and for others which the Spirit makes possible (Rom. 5:5). Thus every Christian at the time of being called to faith (1 Cor. 1:26) is also called to ministry. This is the **general calling of the people of God**; all Christians, in receiving God's grace, hear also God's demand to become transformed into the image of Christ, who is Lord and who is perfect Love.[33]

The report dealt both with 'ecclesial ministries', essential to the building up of the body of Christ, and with Christian calling in the world. It talked of the sense of duty and obligation of the Christian in a secular calling to use their skills to the well-being of human society, adding that, 'from the perspective of faith, **these experiences constitute a vocation from God**'.[34]

The report made complex proposals for the creation of a Methodist Order for Mission and Ministry which would include deaconesses, paid lay workers and voluntary, unpaid workers. These proposals were subsequently abandoned, but they represented an attempt to affirm the importance of lay ministries in the Church. The report aimed to reinforce earlier teaching on the parity of esteem of all styles of ministry. It emphasized that the ministry of the Church could be focused in the collaborative partnership of teams of leaders, lay and 'ministerial' (in the ordained sense), as well as in the individual leadership of ordained persons. It referred to the statement in the 'Lima' Process that ministry should be 'personal, collegial and communal', the last, in particular, indicating the need for leaders always to work in consultation with the people. The use of collaborative team ministry and leadership was seen as a distinctive feature of the Methodist tradition.[35]

The two reports thus rounded off the Methodist reconsideration of the ministry of the Church in the widest sense. They also helped towards the decision finally to develop the category of 'ministers in local appointments', where the candidates concerned would neither itinerate nor be paid, but would serve in their local circuit, often on a part-time basis and sometimes in combination with continuing secular employment.[36]

Cumulatively, the British Methodist achievement in rethinking its theology and practice of ministry between 1960 and 1990 was impressive. It deserves wider appreciation and reception from ecumenical partners. Methodism itself needs to recognize more fully the ecclesiological achievement represented in the work concerned. Fundamental to the ecclesiology concerned was an appreciation of the Church as the 'sign' of God's love and mission in the world, transcending the functional/ontological division which has been as real, if not as clearly recognized, in ecclesiology as in the theology of ministry. The evangelical and missionary origins of Methodism naturally encouraged Methodists to think in terms of the present activity of the Church rather than reflecting on its abiding significance as 'sign', owned and used by God despite the deficiencies of both its ministers and its members.

If there is an area in which Methodist ecclesial awareness continues to be weak, it is in the sense of the Church's continuity across the whole of the Christian era. Methodists have often lacked much awareness of the richness of the Church's history between apostolic times and the age of the Wesleys and even of developments, Methodist and otherwise, between the age of the Wesleys and their own time. More reflection on this might illuminate for Methodists the value of the concept of the sign of the episcopal succession as a constant reminder of the whole of the Tradition. Understanding it as 'sign, but not guarantee' would save Methodists from having to accept any unrealistic view of episcopacy as something that has necessarily always 'worked' well or even better in practice than other systems of

church government. Nor would it commit them to any view
that a church without bishops cannot be an authentic church,
owned and used by a gracious God.

Methodism has preserved, in its understanding of the partnership of lay people, with their own very real and various ministries, and ordained ministers, a balance which other mainstream
churches are seeking. All the mainstream Western churches,
Catholic and Protestant, want an active laity, led and equipped
by the clergy, but also capable of bold and independent service
in Church and world. Methodism, in its theology and practice
combines this partnership with a genuinely universal outlook.
Ministers and people alike are called to have a 'connexional'
sense which is more than just a matter of having a wider perspective of British Methodism as a whole. It implies a concern for
the entire world parish, one that includes all the other churches,
of whatever tradition, and their global sphere of mission. In the
expanding development of their sense of global and ecumenical
responsibility, Methodists will find valuable resources in the
material just surveyed.

Summary, Conclusions, Prospects

No one can, of course, forecast the exact future for Methodist ecclesiology. We cannot tell within what new, and possibly unexpected, contexts future developments may be forged. *Called to Love and Praise* pointed out that British Methodism might well cease to exist as a separate church within the course of the present century.[1] Even if this does not happen, continuing ecumenical fellowship and challenges will probably lead Methodists to examine anew aspects of their ecclesiology which have remained hitherto rather neglected. Chapter 2 of this book contains a clear challenge to re-explore and re-receive elements of Methodist ecclesiology that have most definitely not been at the forefront of Methodist thought in the twentieth century.

The statement on 'Episkope and Episcopacy', adopted by the British Conference in 2000, represents an important example of the re-examination of part of the Methodist ecclesiological heritage in the light of the exigencies of the current ecumenical situation.[2] The Conference of 1997 asked the Faith and Order Committee to examine the Methodist position on episkope (oversight) and episcopacy and to draft a statement for possible adoption which would guide Methodist negotiators in ecumenical conversations across the three countries of Britain and would also help Methodists reflect upon their own practice and experience of oversight. *Called to Love and Praise* had said relatively little about both oversight and episcopacy.[3]

The report was concerned to examine the pragmatic working of episkope in Methodism and not to make any facile assumption that theological theory necessarily determined practice exactly. It emphasized the final authority of Conference, dating

right back to Wesley's deed of 1784, while also stressing that
both the composition of Conference and the exact manner of
the exercise of its power had changed considerably over two
centuries.[4] Adopting from the ecumenical document, *Baptism,
Eucharist, Ministry*, the categorization of episkope as 'personal,
collegial and communal', it examined the different forms of
'episkope' within Methodism at all levels from the local church
to the connexional.[5] It emphasized the importance of the
communal element in episkope within Methodism. It also
pointed to the existence of key elements of collegial episkope,
for example, within the ministerial and diaconal sessions of
Conference, within circuit staff meetings and within local
preachers' meetings.[6] It underlined the very real personal episkope still exercised by superintendent ministers. It gave an interesting account of the changing nature of the episkope of Chairs
of Districts and commented on the problems of adequate episkope within and over the 'Connexional Team', in the light of
the very considerable restructuring of the mid-nineties.[7] Even
more recently, a 'Leadership Task Group' has been examining
the nature of leadership in Methodism and questioning possible
lacunae. It has suggested that Methodism might have something
to learn from secular management models and has raised the
question of an overall coordinator for the 'Connexional Team'.[8]

On the question of episcopacy, the report summarized previous Methodist statements on the matter and examined various
models of episcopacy as practised both within other traditions
and within sister Methodist churches overseas.[9] It then offered
a series of guidelines, summarizing the current state of oversight
within Methodism, referring to the values that current practice
seemed to encapsulate and pointing to the conditions under
which British Methodism would feel able to 'receive the sign of
the episcopal succession'.[10] It was made quite clear that
Methodism valued all three forms of episkope, but that it particularly believed that 'personal episkope . . . should be exercised
within a collegial or communal context'. It emphasized that
episcopacy could be adopted provided it did not involve
Methodism in repudiating its past and provided 'all ministries,

including those of oversight are exercised *within* the ministry of the whole people of God and at its service, rather than in isolation from it and supremacy over it'.[11] It counselled, however, against any immediate unilateral adoption of episcopacy by British Methodism, arguing that its reception should occur within the context of appropriate ecumenical developments, a clause which, however, the Conference then deleted.[12] It may well be that Methodism will adopt episcopacy in Wales and/or Scotland ahead of England, since in both countries negotiations involving episcopal churches are advanced.[13] In England, the Common Statement of the Formal Conversations between the Methodist Church of Great Britain and the Church of England, issued in December 2001, has recommended the establishment of a new 'covenant relationship between the two churches, involving their mutual recognition as authentic churches'.[14] The question of ministerial reconciliation and interchangeability has, however, been deferred to a later stage.

The Conference adopted the guidelines of the episcopacy and episkope report and commended the report for study at district, circuit and local level. The Faith and Order Committee will report on comments received to the Conference of 2002. It is, of course, possible that the report may then be amended. In the meantime, it is a valuable tool for ongoing Methodist reflection. It can be argued that it is a valuable witness to Tradition; it certainly underlines and reaffirms the Methodist emphasis, reaching right back to Wesley, on the importance of proper oversight as integral to the Church's life. It also raises questions about the way in which that oversight is currently practised. Finally, it directs Methodists to think about how their system of oversight might accommodate and conceivably be enriched by personal episcopacy within the historic succession without impugning the Methodist emphasis upon communal oversight.

Further challenges may confidently be expected from Methodism's dialogue partners. The most recent report of the international Roman Catholic–Methodist dialogue Commission, *Speaking the Truth in Love*, deals with what is perhaps the thorniest ecumenical question of all, that of teaching authority.

In it, both churches challenge each other about the nature and range of their teaching activity and authority. Methodists are called on to explain the exact extent 'to which they ascribe authority to the doctrinal statements of the Conferences'. They are asked how they understand this authority in relation to that of Scripture and the other elements of the 'Wesleyan Quadrilateral'. They are asked to justify the involvement of lay people in such decision making. Both dialogue partners make strong statements about the guidance of the Spirit in the teaching mission of the Church. These need addressing in the context of the theological pluralism of Methodism, and, indeed, much of the rest of the Church. Years of work lie ahead on this topic, made complex by the simultaneous continued insistence of the Orthodox and Roman Catholic churches on the infallibility of the Church coupled with the emergence of the totally countervailing philosophy of postmodernism with its extreme relativism. The discussion of such questions will have to address the need to balance clear and authoritative proclamation of the fundamentals of the gospel against the necessity of ensuring legitimate freedom of theological exploration in a changing world.[15]

The report particularly calls for more work on 'the relationship between ordination, authoritative teaching and the sure guidance of the Holy Spirit'.[16] Further questions about the nature of Methodist presbyteral ministry come from a recent consultation, entitled, 'What is a Presbyter?'.[17]

Yet more challenges and agenda items come from the proposed Anglican–Methodist Covenant, already briefly mentioned above. The proposed Covenant would involve the two churches in making seven affirmations about each other and six commitments to common action. The affirmations involve mutual recognition as 'true churches belonging to the One, Holy, Catholic and Apostolic Church of Jesus Christ'. They go on to affirm each other's apostolicity of faith and sacramental life and each other's lay and ordained ministries. They end with an affirmation of the conciliar and connexional nature of both churches and the significant statement that 'there already exists a basis for agreement on the principles of episcopal oversight as a visible sign and instrument of the communion of the Church in time and space'.

This final affirmation offers a basis on which future conversations can be held in an endeavour to find a way forward for mutual interchangeability of ministries and fully organic unity. The commitments are related to the necessary process of growing into closer unity that would need to precede any future steps. There is a commitment to mutual reception of insights and riches, especially encapsulated in the wording of the second affirmation, which talks of sharing 'the distinctive contributions of our traditions', and the fifth affirmation, 'We commit ourselves to listen to each other and to take account of each other's concerns, especially in areas that affect our relationship as churches.' Finally, there is the commitment to the gradual development of structures of joint oversight, 'on the way to a fully united ministry of oversight'.[18]

The main remaining problem will, undoubtedly be that of the establishment of a fully interchangeable ministry. The delicate question of opening up episcopal ministry to women is also identified. Methodism insists that all ministries be open equally to men and women; the Church of England has yet to decide to open the episcopate to women. Many Methodists will wonder why, given the affirmation of existing ministries proposed in the draft covenant, it will not be possible to establish immediate interchangeability in its wake. Many may wonder why the established precedent of the Church of South India, where, at inauguration in 1947, all existing presbyters, whether or not episcopally ordained, were equally accepted as presbyters of the new church, is not being recommended. The idea of establishing a covenant, followed by further negotiations to lead to full interchangeability of ministry owes much to the precedent established in Anglican agreements with non-episcopal churches in France and Germany and an overriding strategy of 'unity by stages'.[19]

A welcome feature of the report is the care with which issues of ecclesiology and ministry have been examined. The report also points to the very considerable degree of diversity of theological opinion and practice within both churches.[20] It could certainly be argued that no closer relationship between them is likely to be fruitful without honest acceptance of this as a fact of life for the Pilgrim Church. The whole question of the extent of legitimate and enriching diversity within the Universal Church remains the $64,000 question of ecumenism. Anglicans and Methodists in tandem may have a vital contribution to make to this debate in the course of a common exploration, within the prospective covenant relationship, of this issue.

All these matters will need the most patient consideration in both churches. Methodists can feel that Anglicans have moved a long way from some of the more rigid positions of yesteryear towards the sort of mutual recognition for which the classical Wesleyans called even if they have not yet moved quite as far as Methodists might hope.

This book has attempted to illustrate the complex evolution of Methodist ecclesiology. Amid all the change, can we say that there are any enduring characteristics of Methodist ecclesiology? In particular, are there any that we might commend for wider study and possible reception within the Oikoumene?

One can argue that there are three enduring principles underlying Methodist ecclesiology. The first and most important is the understanding of the interdependent nature of the Church at every level. The Church is, above all, a communion, a sharing in God's gifts, in his Spirit, in the vision of the Kingdom of which the Church is the herald, and, in some sense, the foretaste. It is a partnership in proclamation, celebration and embodied witness; we are, as Charles Wesley put it, 'partners of like blessed faith'.[21] Methodists rejoice in their fellowship with the saints of all ages, a point emphasized by Charles Wesley and Benjamin Gregory alike.[22] Methodists are interconnected, interdependent and mutually accountable at every level, though their practice of this interconnectedness is, of course, imperfect in this world.

Methodism has sought to embody this experience, insight and principle at every level in the 'connexional principle'. It is important to stress that it is a principle. The precise structures of connexionalism are, rightly, subject to constant adaptation. Some may well think they have been subject to too much constant chopping and changing within the last twenty-five years or so, but that is an issue for debate. In the past, Methodists have tended to think of the 'connexional principle' as a Methodist 'peculiar institution'. Perhaps now the time has come for Methodists to commend the principle more widely, particularly in an era when all the other major traditions are recovering the concept of *koinonia* as central ecclesiologically.

In this context, the recent report of the 'trilateral' conversations between the Church of England, the United Reformed Church and British Methodism is interesting. The report asserts that all three churches can be said to be connexional, but in different ways. Methodists are pleased to discover other ways in which the 'connexional principle' can be embodied and to explore ways in which they might contribute to a more rounded connexionalism for Methodism. The two partner churches affirmed their desire to explore the Methodist understanding of connexionalism further. Their representatives 'sought further explanation of what it meant to say that the connexional principle enshrined a vital truth about the nature of the Church'.[23] This would seem to promise a dialogue in which all three churches try to advance their common understanding of ecclesiology, learning from and receiving from each other.

British Methodism faces two challenges on its practice of connexionalism, the first an explicit one from our American Methodist sisters and brothers, the second, an implicit one from Christians in the 'catholic' traditions. American Methodism practises 'global' connexionalism and the quadrennial General Conference of the United Methodist Church includes representatives from the United Methodist Church in other parts of the world. American Methodists can ask, and indeed have asked, why the British Methodist concept of connexionalism seems to stop at national frontiers and results in the creation of totally autonomous churches rather than churches retaining links of real mutual accountability.[24] It is a fair question.

Roman Catholics and Anglicans, as they come to know Methodism better, may well discern that, though our connexional structures enable enviably close mutual accountability between the churches of today, they do not always as adequately express the continuity and communion of the churches across time. They may well argue that the adoption by Methodism of the sign of the episcopal succession will help Methodism to a richer sense of its relationship with the whole Church across the ages. I think it undeniable that, in general, Roman Catholics, Anglicans and Orthodox do have a richer sense of such continuity than is usually the case with Methodists, who often have little sense of their own past, let alone that of the rest of the Church. One encounters those for whom church history is largely a matter of Acts, followed by a long gap, Mr Wesley on horseback, followed by another long gap till they reach times they can themselves remember. This is a caricature, but it contains an ounce of truth. In the opinion of the present writer the conditions are propitious for an enrichment of the Methodist sense of *koinonia* across time, especially since the best Roman Catholic and Anglican thinking now accepts a theology of *koinonia* which stresses, as Methodist theology has done for a long time, that all ministries are exercised within the total fellowship of the Church, at its service and not in isolation from it or above it.[25]

The second great emphasis in Methodist ecclesiology is upon a generous recognition of all communities that clearly carry the marks of the Spirit as true churches whatever their precise ordering. Wesley argued that it would be an absurdity to unchurch the continental Protestants because they lacked the episcopal succession.[26] Gregory was even more trenchant in his attacks on those who unchurched other Christian communities.[27] Methodism has always repudiated an 'independent' ecclesiology as inadequate, while not denying that churches thus organized are true local churches within the Universal Body of Christ. Methodism has always argued that it is the possession and expression of apostolic faith and life that is fundamental. Writers from Jackson to Slater and Quick endeavoured to show the similarity between the nature and fruits of the apostolic and the Wesleyan missions.[28] The 'Baptism, Eucharist, Ministry' Process of the World Council of Churches argued that apostolicity depended upon a whole bundle of characteristics and not primarily upon ministerial succession, though the latter could act as a valuable sign of continuity. Paragraph M34 of *Baptism, Eucharist, Ministry* states:

> Apostolic tradition in the Church means continuity in the permanent characteristics of the Church of the apostles; witness to the apostolic faith, proclamation and fresh interpretation of the Gospel, celebration of baptism and the eucharist, the transmission of ministerial responsibilities, communion in prayer, love, joy and suffering, service to the sick and needy, unity among the local churches and sharing the gifts which the Lord has given to each.[29]

Methodist studies, such as those of W. F. Slater, *Methodism in the Light of the Early Church*, and W. A. Quick, *Methodism, a Parallel*, could almost be seen as commentaries, in anticipation, upon the Lima text.[30] Where apostolicity exists in terms of all the other characteristics, it can scarcely be denied to a church solely on the grounds of a breach in episcopal or presbyteral succession.

Modern Anglican ecclesiology has begun to take this point seriously and has acted upon it in the 'Porvoo', 'Meissen' and 'Reuilly' agreements, acknowledging the apostolicity and authenticity of churches and ministries that still lack the 'sign of the episcopal succession'.[31] Roman Catholic thinking has yet to make this jump, though there are signs that many Catholic theologians are exploring the possibility of the recognition of the apostolic authenticity of churches that have kept the apostolic faith and witness while not having an episcopally ordered ministry.[32]

The final point to stress is the Methodist tradition of willingness to explore the gifts that others have to offer. Freed from any heritage of taking absolutist stands on church order, whether 'independent', presbyterian or episcopal, Methodism has proved able to explore the gifts on offer from others. In many joint URC/Methodist churches, Methodists have entered into the reformed heritage of eldership, the general relevance of which has been further explored in such forums as the URC/Methodist joint committee and the 'informal' tripartite conversations alluded to above. Methodism has now three times, in 1969–72, in 1982 and in 2000, shown itself willing to embrace the sign of the episcopal succession within the context of a scheme for closer unity. The thorny question of the 'Petrine ministry' has been discussed in the international Roman Catholic–Methodist Commission with Methodists effectively inviting Catholics to 'prove' the relevance of such a ministry to the effective unity of the Church, whereupon Methodism would have to take it seriously.[33]

Pace my cautious remarks at the beginning of this chapter, the future for Methodist ecclesiology would seem to lie, above all, in sensitive dialogue with our ecumenical partners, in the course of which Methodists would, as Shrewsbury hoped, become both receivers and givers. There is, perhaps, still substance in his hope that Methodism might become the 'middle bond of union', not just, as he originally envisaged, between Anglicans and the other 'free churches', but more widely between the churches of 'catholic' order and the churches that major on their Reformation or free church heritages.[34] A sensitively adapted 'connexionalism' can, as has already been asserted, reconcile and find place for due local congregational freedom alongside responsible and accountable membership of the Church Universal. It can reconcile the personal, collegial and communal elements in episkope. It can balance a recognition of the value of historic continuity alongside a recognition of the authentic life in the Spirit wherever found. It can manifest the nature of the Church as communion, across space and time, in true partnership between ordained ministers and layfolk.

Methodism can be a real 'bridge' church. It identifies neither with the extremes of congregational autonomy and independence nor with hierarchicalism. It sees the Church as a communion of love in which all are called both to give and to receive. The very concept of communion renders untenable any idea of authority as simply emanating from the 'top down' or the 'bottom up'. Rather, there is, as both Gregory and the German Roman Catholic J. A. Mohler argued, a 'circulation of love', 'an embodied love' within which the insights, charisms and con-tributions of all have their due place.[35]

In a very real sense Methodism is committed, both by its claims and its experience, to the utmost generosity in giving and receiving within the Universal Church. The constant emphasis within Methodism, from Wesley's famous sermon to the claims in the Deed of Union and the more recent assertions of *Called to Love and Praise* upon catholicity of spirit commits the Methodist people to serious ecclesiological and ecumenical exploration alongside her sister trinitarian churches.[36] Methodism rejoices in its distinctiveness as a gift given precisely to be shared within the yet richer and wider fellowship of the Church catholic. The breadth of the 'Wesleyan Quadrilateral' with its acknowledge-ment of the authority of Tradition, reason and experience along-side the primary authority of Scripture, commits Methodism to the widest possible dialogue with others. The 'disinterestedness' and humility commanded by Shrewsbury commit Methodists to unprejudiced and constant re-reception of the Apostolic Faith. This 'disinterestedness' is reflected in the 'Common Statement' of the Anglican–Methodist conversations. The central para-graph of the proposed 'covenant' statement reads,

> We do so [covenant] in a spirit of penitence for all that human sinfulness and narrowness of vision have contributed to our past divisions, believing that we have been impoverished through our separation and that our witness to the Gospel has been weakened accordingly, and in a spirit of thanks-giving and joy for the convergence in faith and collaboration in mission that we have experienced in recent years.[37]

The task of Methodism in both mission and unity remains unfinished.

Notes

Introduction

1. D. Kirkpatrick (ed.), *The Doctrine of the Church*, London: Epworth, 1964, p. 11.

2. B. Gregory, *The Holy Catholic Church*, London, 1873 (hereafter cited as *HCC*); Gregory's other significant work is *A Handbook of Scriptural Church Principles*, London: Wesleyan Conference Office, 1888, written at the request of the Wesleyan Conference (hereafter cited as *Handbook*).

3. Rigg's main works cited here are *The Connexional Economy of Wesleyan Methodism in its Ecclesiastical and Spiritual Aspects*, London: Wesleyan Conference Office, 1852/1878, and *A Comparative View of Church Organisations, Primitive and Protestant. With a supplement on Methodist secessions and Methodist union*, London: Charles Kelly, 3rd edn, 1897. Hereafter respectively cited as *Economy* and *View*.

4. See his observations in G. Tavard, 'The Dialogue between Methodists and Catholics', *One in Christ*, 30, 2 (1994), pp. 176–83 (180).

5. Discussed in detail in ch. 1.

6. J. M. Turner, *Conflict and Reconciliation: Studies in Methodism and Ecumenism in England, 1740–1982*, London, Epworth 1985, p. 80.

7. Gregory, *Handbook*, vol. 2, p. 256.

8. The designation used in the classic *Large Hymnbook* of 1780, thereafter reprinted in later Wesleyan hymn books till 1877. Hymns, nos 478–539.

9. On US Methodism, see Thomas E. Frank, *Polity, Practice and Mission of the United Methodist Church*, Nashville: Abingdon, 1997. For some comparison of the concept of connexionalism in the two churches, see B. Robbins and D. Carter, 'Connexionalism and Koinonia: A Wesleyan Contribution to Ecclesiology', *One in Christ*, 34, 4 (1998), pp. 320–36.

10. *Called to Love and Praise: A Methodist Conference Statement on the Church*, Peterborough: Methodist Publishing House, 1999.

1 The Ecclesiological Heritage of the Wesleys and the First Methodists

1. R. Heitzenrater, *Wesley and the People Called Methodists*, Nashville: Abingdon, 1995. See especially the introductory remarks, pp. ix–xii.

2. The best overall study of Wesley and his movement is H. Rack, *Reasonable Enthusiast: John Wesley and the Rise of Methodism*, London: Epworth, 1989.

3. Rigg, *View*, p. 207.

4. Rigg, *View*, pp. 207–20. R. E. Davies, A. R. George and G. Rupp (eds), *A History of the Methodist Church in Great Britain*, 4 vols (hereafter cited as *History*), London: Epworth, 1965–88, vol. 4, p. 92; cited also in Gregory, *Handbook*, vol. 2, p. 65.

5. J. H. Rigg, *The Relations of John Wesley and of Wesleyan Methodism to the Church of England, Investigated and Explained*, London: Longmans Green & Co., 1868. See esp. p. 28, where Rigg claims that Wesley's espousal of the doctrine of justification by faith, and his consequent mission, meant that he was compelled to 'abandon his dearly beloved ground of High Church Ritualism and exclusiveness, and to become the head of a religious community founded and organised upon the principles of free religious life'. See pp. 39–62 for detailed justification of this view and for Rigg's belief that the Conference, after Wesley's death, followed strictly the principles of the founder as Rigg understood them!

6. For Methodism in the 1790s and the disputes at the time of the 'Plan of Pacification', see J. Walsh, 'Methodism at the End of the Eighteenth Century', in Davies and Rupp (eds), *History*, vol. 1, pp. 275–316.

7. J. Wesley, *Works of Rev. John Wesley*, ed. F. Baker, 13 vols, Nashville: Abingdon, 1986. 'A Plain Account of the People Called Methodists', vol. 9, pp. 254–80 (259).

8. Cited in H. Bett, *The Spirit of Methodism*, London: Epworth, 1937, p. 79.

9. J. Telford, (ed.), *Letters of John Wesley*, 8 vols, London: Epworth, 1931, vol. 8, p. 267.

10. See e.g. the hymns in Part V, nos 478–539 of the classical *Large Hymn Book* of 1780, as constantly then reproduced in subsequent Wesleyan hymn books down to that of 1877. A version with scholarly apparatus is contained in Wesley, *Works*, vol. 7. See *Hymns and Psalms*, London: Methodist Publishing House, 1983, the present official Methodist hymn book, nos 752–63, for some perennially popular hymns of this genre.

11. *Hymns and Psalms* (hereafter cited as *HP*), 756. See also D. Carter, 'Church and Praise in the hymnody of the Wesleys', *Sobornost*, NS 18, 1 (1996), pp. 30–47.

12. For a good short study of Wesley's ecclesiology, see C. Williams,

John Wesley's Theology Today, London: Epworth, 1960, pp. 141–66. See reference 4, above, for the quotation referred to.

13. Wesley, *Works*, vol,. 9, p. 263.

14. Rigg, *Churchmanship*, pp. 26–8, where he discusses the 'sons of Korah' sermon, which can be found in Wesley, *Works*, vol. 4, pp. 75–84, under the title of 'Prophets and Priests'. Rigg effectively attributes this 'aberration', as he sees it, to impending senility.

15. F. Baker, *John Wesley and the Church of England*, London: Epworth, 1970; E. W. Thompson, *Wesley, Apostolic Man*, London: Epworth, 1957; F. Hunter, *John Wesley and the Coming Comprehensive Church*, London: Epworth, 1968; A. B. Lawson, *John Wesley and the Christian Ministry: The Sources and Development of His Opinions and Practice*, London: SPCK, 1963; Williams, *Wesley's Theology*; Rack, *Enthusiast*.

16. Hunter, *Coming*, pp. 9–53.

17. Williams, *Wesley's Theology*, pp. 141–66.

18. Lawson, *Ministry*, pp. 47–70, for the influence of Edward Stillingfleet and King upon Wesley; pp. 71–98, for further development in Wesley's views.

19. Rack, *Enthusiast*, pp. 506–25, for Wesley's ordinations. Gregory, *Handbook*, vol. 2, p. 102, for Wesley's remark about leaving the American brethren to the 'Scriptures and the Primitive Church'.

20. Wesley quotation from Sermon 107, *Works*, vol. 3, p. 511. Even Rigg admits that Wesley wanted to avoid separation, however much he may have feared its inevitability. 'His object was not division or separation, but revival and re-animation.' Cf. also Wesley in his 'Reasons against a separation from the Church of England': 'We should not act in direct contradiction to that very end for which we believe God has raised us up. The chief design of his Providence in sending us out was undoubtedly to quicken our brethren. And the first message of all our preachers is to the lost sheep of the Church of England' (Wesley, *Works*, vol. 9, p. 336).

21. T. Runyon, *The New Creation: John Wesley's Theology Today*, Nashville: Abingdon, 1998, p. 107.

22. For the concept of Methodism as an order within the Church catholic, see G. Wainwright, *The Ecumenical Moment: Crisis and Opportunity for the Church*, Grand Rapids: Eerdmans, 1983, pp 196–99. For the sermon on the 'Catholic Spirit', Wesley, *Works*, vol. 2, pp. 81–95.

23. Wesley, Sermon 75, 'On Schism', *Works*, vol. 3, pp. 59–69 (65) for first two quotations given; 'Reasons against a separation from the Church of England', *Works*, vol. 9, pp. 334–9 (335) for the last quotation.

24. Runyon, *New Creation*, pp. 102–7.

25. D. Lowes Watson, *The Early Methodist Class Meeting, Its Origins and Significance*, Nashville: Discipleship Resources, 1985.

26. R. George Eli, *Social Holiness: John Wesley's Thinking on Christian Community and Its Relationship to the Social Order*, New York: Peter Lang, 1993, p. 64. For Dale's criticism of Wesley, see R. W. Dale, *The Evangelical Revival and other sermons*, London: Hodder and Stoughton, 1880, pp. 1–40. For Wesley on 'social holiness', see preface to the 1739 Hymn Book cited in G. Osborn, (ed.), *Poetical Works of John and Charles Wesley*, 12 vols, London: Wesleyan Conference Office, 1868, vol. 1, p. xxii.

27. Eli, *Social Holiness*, p. 81.

28. Eli, *Social Holiness*, pp. 54–5.

29. Eli, *Social Holiness*, pp. 58–9.

30. See, e.g., *God's Reign and Our Unity*, the report of the Anglican–Reformed International Commission, 1984, paras 29–34, cited in J. Gros, H. Meyer and W. Rusch, *Growth in Agreement II: Reports and Agreed Statements of Ecumenical Conversations on a World Level*, Geneva: WCC; Grand Rapids: Eerdmans, 2000, pp. 114–54 (123–4).

31. Lawson, *Ministry*, pp. 74–5.

32. Gregory, *Handbook*, vol. 1, p. 98, actually argues that variation in order is not merely permissible but even necessary under certain circumstances.

33. Davies, George and Rupp (eds), *History*, vol. 4, p. 84.

34. Rack, *Enthusiast*, pp. 296–305; p. 518 for Charles's attack on John's 1784 ordinations.

35. Wesley, *Works*, vol. 3, sermon 112, 'On Laying the Foundation at City Road', pp. 577–93, especially pp. 585–6.

36. Rack, *Enthusiast*, p. 299, for Wesley's observation that he had more problems with 'soul-damning clergy than with soul-saving laymen'.

37. Wesley, *Works*, vol. 2, sermon 39, 'The Catholic Spirit', pp. 81–95, esp. pp. 92–3.

38. Wesley, *Works*, Sermons, vol. 3, p. 585.

39. See, e.g., the four linked hymns for the Love Feast, nos 519–22 in the classic *Large Hymn Book* of 1780.

40. Sermon 104, 'On Attending the Church Service', in Wesley, *Works*, vol. 3, pp. 464–78 (477).

41. For the sheer breadth of inspiration drawn by Wesley from diverse continental European sources, see the essay by J. Orcibal, 'The Theological Originality of John Wesley and Continental Spirituality', in Davies, George and Rupp (eds), *History*, vol. 1 pp. 81–119. For Wesley's emphasis upon the Lord's Supper, afterwards much attenuated in nineteenth- and early twentieth-century Methodism, see J. Bowmer, *Sacrament of the Lord's Supper in Early Methodism*, London: Dacre, 1951.

42. Cited in Lawson, *Ministry*, p. 75.

43. For Wesley and Rome, see the standard work, D. Butler, *Methodists*

and Papists, London: Darton, Longman and Todd, 1995. On the two matters mentioned specifically here, see Rack, *Enthusiast*, pp. 305–13. Wesley, *Works*, vol. 3, sermon 74, 'Of the Church', pp. 45–57 (52), 'whoever they are who have one Spirit, one hope, one faith, one God and Father of all, I can, I can easily bear with their holding wrong opinions, yea and even superstitious ones'.

44. Wesley, *Works*, vol. 9, p. 259.

45. Rack, *Enthusiast*, pp. 246–50, for context. Full text cited in L. Tyerman, *Life and Times of Rev. John Wesley, M.A., founder of the methodises*, 3 vols, London: Hodder and Stoughton, 2nd edn, 1871–6, 1876, vol. 2, p. 578.

46. Wesley, *Works*, vol. 3, Sermon 97, 'On the Duty of Obedience to Pastors', pp. 374–83 (374).

47. Davies, George and Rupp (eds), *History*, vol. 4, p. 91.

48. Lawson, *Ministry*, pp. 75, 80. This emphasis upon effectiveness as a proof of authenticity became a key part of later Wesleyan apologetics and tradition. Cf. Thomas Jackson in his 1850 sermon on *Christian Presbyters, Their Office, Duties and Reward*, London: John Mason, 1850: p. 29: 'that you are true elders is manifest from the very existence and character of those societies, for the seal of your eldership is "those in the Lord"'.

49. Lawson, *Ministry*, pp. 85–8; Rigg, *Churchmanship*, pp. 53–7.

50. On connexionalism and its present relevance, see B. Beck, 'Some Reflections on Connexionalism', *Epworth Review*, 18, 2/3 (1991), no. 2, pp. 48–59, no. 3, pp. 43–50; Robbins and Carter, 'Connexionalism and Koinonia', *One in Christ*, 34, 4 (1998), pp. 320–36.

51. Rack notes Wesley's determination also to avoid pure sectarianism. 'It was the sectarianism of Dissent that Wesley feared and resisted' (Rack, *Enthusiast*, p. 249). See also H. Rack, *The Future of John Wesley's Methodism*, London: Lutterworth, 1965, pp. 17–18.

52. Citation from 'Twelve Rules of a Helper', quoted in J. S. Simon (ed.), *A Summary of Methodist Law and Discipline*, London: Methodist Publishing House, 1923, p. 272, and in Davies, George and Rupp (eds), *History*, vol. 4, p. 118.

53. T. Campbell, *John Wesley and Christian Antiquity: Religious Vision and Cultural Change*, Nashville: Abingdon, 1991.

54. *HP*, 756.

55. Osborne (ed.), *Poetical Works*, vol. 5, p. 480.

56. *The Methodist Hymn Book*, London: Methodist Publishing House, 1904, no. 687.

57. Osborne (ed.), *Poetical Works*, vol. 5, p. 228.

58. *The Methodist Hymn Book*, London: Methodist Publishing House, 1933, no. 720. This verse is omitted from *HP*, 764.

59. *HP*, 753.

60. *HP*, 300.
61. *HP*, 773.
62. *HP*, 374.
63. *Methodist Hymn Book*, 1933, no. 717.
64. *HP*, 764.
65. See ref. 43 above. For a general consideration of Wesley's reactions to Catholic saints and spirituality see, Butler, *Methodists and Papists*, chs 12/13, pp. 135–40 and 141–59.
66. See, e.g., 'A Short Method of converting all the Roman Catholics in the Kingdom of Ireland: Humbly proposed to the Bishops and clergy of that kingdom', *Works of Rev. J. Wesley*, London: Wesleyan Methodist Book Room, no date, vol. 10, pp. 129–32.
67. Cited in Wainwright, *Ecumenical Moment*, p. 211. Wesley's letter to 'John Smith' of 25 June 1746.
68. See ch. 2, esp. my discussion of the ecclesiology of Benjamin Gregory (pp. 52–3).
69. Rack, *Enthusiast*, pp. 506–16. For Charles's reaction, p. 518.
70. Rack, *Enthusiast*, pp. 502–6.
71. Wesley, *Works*, vol. 9, pp. 538–40.

2 Classical Wesleyan Ecclesiology

1. The standard work on the doctrine of the 'pastoral office' is J. C. Bowmer, *Pastor and People: A Study of Church and Ministry in Wesleyan Methodism from the Death of John Wesley (1791) to the Death of Jabez Bunting (1858)*, London: Epworth, 1975. R. Currie, *Methodism Divided: A Study in the Sociology of Ecumenicalism*, London: Faber and Faber, 1968, provides a good overview of Methodist divisions and the factors at play in them. Turner, *Conflict*, is good on the changing nature of Anglican–Methodist relationships.
2. The best overall account of Methodism in this period is in Davies, George and Rupp (eds), *History*, vol. 1, ch. 11; vol. 2, throughout.
3. J. Kent, *Jabez Bunting, the Last Wesleyan*, London: Epworth, 1955, gives a particularly clear and succinct account of the differences between 'high' and 'low' Methodism in their understanding of ministry.
4. See, e.g., J. Benson, *An Apology for the people called Methodists*, London: Cordeux, 1812.
5. See, e.g., W. J. Shrewsbury, *An Essay on the Scriptural Character of the Wesleyan Methodist Economy*, London: Renshaw and Kirkman, 1840, and, in particular, ch. 5, pp. 99–147, on the relationship of Methodism to the Establishment.
6. For the Wesleyan sense of solidarity, see especially the anonymous, *Methodism in 1879: Impressions of the Wesleyan Church and its Ministers,*

London: Haughton & Co., 1879, p. 137. For the quotation from Gregory, see *Handbook*, vol. 2, p. 256.

7. Turner, *Conflict*, pp. 146–72, deals with the Oxford Movement and Methodist reactions to it.

8. For a good account of the feelings of many layfolk, especially lay officials in the Wesleyan Church, see M. Batty, *Stages in the Development and Control of Wesleyan Lay Leadership, 1791–1878*, Peterborough: Methodist Publishing House, 1988, esp. chs 4 and 12. For Independent criticisms and a Wesleyan refutation of them, see esp. Rigg, *Economy*, esp. pp. 36–54, where Rigg cites 'Independent' evidence against the deficiencies of their own system.

9. For Jackson, see T. Jackson, *Recollections of My Own Life and Times*, London: Wesleyan Conference Office, 1873; also his *Christian Presbyters*.

10. A. Barrett, *An Essay on the Pastoral Office*, London: John Mason, 1839, *The Ministry and Polity of the Christian Church*, London: John Mason, 1854.

11. For a brief introduction to Rigg, see D. Carter, *James H. Rigg*, Peterborough: Foundery Press, 1994.

12. W. F. Slater, *Methodism in the Light of the Early Church*, London: T. Woolmer, 1885; W. A. Quick, *Methodism, a Parallel*, London: T. Woolmer, 1889.

13. R. Watson, *Theological Institutes*, 3 vols, London: John Mason, 1828; also in *Works of Richard Watson*, 12 vols, London: John Mason, 1830, vol. 12, pp. 166–211. W. B. Pope, *A Compendium of Christian Theology*, 3 vols, London: Wesleyan Conference Office, 2nd edn rev. and enlarged, 1880, vol. 3, pp. 259–364.

14. Slater, *Methodism in the Light of the Early Church*, p. 137.

15. B. Beck, 'Some Reflections on Connexionalism'. Robbins and Carter, 'Connexionalism and Koinonia'.

16. Rigg, *View*, p. 2.

17. Rigg, *Economy*, p. 6.

18. Rigg, *Economy*, p. 6.

19. Gregory, *HCC*, pp. 213–88.

20. Barrett, *Ministry*, p. 239.

21. Rigg, *Economy*, pp. 170–1.

22. This seminal Conference declaration will be cited in the section on interchurch relationships and unity: see p. 51.

23. Shrewsbury, *Scriptural Character*, pp. 94–9.

24. Rigg, *View*, p. 207.

25. Rigg, *View*, p. 29, where he argues that if there had been a divinely intended prescriptive form of church government, it would have been clearly indicated in the New Testament. He continues: 'the slight, cursory

and obscure character of the notices relating to the subject actually found in Acts are quite incompatible with the idea of a divinely prescribed model of church organisation'.

26. J. Dixon, *Methodism in its Origin, Economy and Present Position*, London: John Mason, 1843, pp. 74–5.

27. Shrewsbury, *Scriptural Character*, pp. 76, 78, 94, 96.

28. Watson, *Institutes*, vol. 3, pp. 414–59, for his general ecclesiology. In common with other Wesleyan ecclesiologists Watson stressed the purpose of the Church as primary above any concept of exact structure. Cf. his very Wesleyan sentiment on p. 422: 'in those particulars in which they were left free by Scriptures, the primitive Christians adopted those arrangements for the Church which would render it most efficient'.

29. Pope says that the Church has 'lodged' its authority with the ministry. He does not attempt, as for example does Shrewsbury, to assert a ministerial authority existing prior to the Church. Pope, *Compendium*, vol. 3, p. 345.

30. Gregory, *HCC*, pp. 1–2.

31. Pope, *Compendium*, vol. 3, pp. 266–7; Gregory, *HCC*, pp. 19, 21.

32. J. Zizioulas, *Being as Communion: Studies in Personhood and the Church*, London: Darton, Longman and Todd, 1985.

33. Gregory, *HCC*, p. 15.

34. Pope, *Compendium*, vol. 3, p. 265.

35. Gregory, *HCC*, p. 49.

36. Gregory, *HCC*, p. 57.

37. Pope, *Compendium*, vol. 3, p. 263.

38. Gregory, *HCC*, p. 17.

39. Gregory, *HCC*, p. 196.

40. Gregory, *HCC*, p. 195–6.

41. Gregory, *HCC*, pp. 8, 10.

42. Gregory, *HCC*, pp. 46–7.

43. Gregory, *HCC*, pp. 4–5.

44. Gregory, *HCC*, p. 41.

45. Thus, W. R. Ward, *Religion and Society in England 1790–1850* London: Batsford, 1972, p. 104.

46. In 1771, e.g., during a dispute in Dublin, Wesley had made it quite clear that it was the sole responsibility of the 'assistant', i.e. the travelling preacher, to make final decisions on discipline.

47. Benson's views are cited in Batty, *Stages*, pp. 15–16.

48. Batty, *Stages*, pp. 31–40, for the rules of 1795/7 and some subsequent disputes.

49. Bowmer, *Pastor*, esp. pp. 202–28.

50. Rigg, *Economy*, pp. 24–36, esp. pp. 27, 31.

51. Barrett, *Ministry*, p. 240.

52. S. D. Waddy (1804–76). See biography by his youngest daughter, Adeline Waddy, *The Life of the Rev. S. D. Waddy, DD*, London: Wesleyan Conference Office, 1878. Sermon, 1860, p. 12.

53. See, e.g., Rigg, *View*, pp. 222–3.

54. R. Kissack, *Church or No Church: A Study of the Development of the Concept of Church in British Methodism*, London: Epworth, 1964, p. 88.

55. Shrewsbury, *Scriptural Character*, pp. 150–1.

56. Shrewsbury, *Scriptural Character*, pp. 31–2, 184–5.

57. Shrewsbury, *Scriptural Character*, pp. 184–5.

58. Shrewsbury, *Scriptural Character*, pp. 184–5. Barrett, *Ministry* p. 255, where he is especially concerned to stress the 'principle of a mutual fellowship or union' as constituting the bond of essential equality, despite his concession of the case for a degree of practical primacy in some situations.

59. Barrett, *Ministry*, pp. 246, 255.

60. Barrett, *Ministry*, pp. 24–5, 329.

61. Barrett, *Ministry*, p. 152.

62. Barrett, *Ministry*, p. 369, where he emphasizes the duty of the pastorate to 'raise up and qualify all subordinate agents who teach'. For Barrett, an essential aspect in the difference between 'local' preachers and ministers is that the latter are separated from all secular concerns solely for the work of the gospel.

63. Barrett, *Ministry*, pp. 274, 283–4.

64. T. Jackson, *Wesleyan Methodism, a revival of apostolic Christianity*, London; John Mason, 1839. Gregory, *Handbook*, vol. 1. pp. 83–4.

65. Gregory, *HCC*, p. 103.

66. Rigg, *Economy*, p. 59.

67. Rigg, *View*, pp. 27–8.

68. Rigg, *Economy*, pp. 115–21, 149–60.

69. Barrett, *Ministry*, p. 291, where he talks of the key role in helping to discern the genuineness of the call of ministerial candidates. For his thoughts on Cyprian's practice, see pp. 325–30.

70. Shrewsbury, *Scriptural Character*, p. 225.

71. Shrewsbury, *Scriptural Character*, p. 226.

72. Shrewsbury, *Scriptural Character*, p. 54.

73. Barrett, *Ministry*, p. 333.

74. Gregory, *HCC*, pp. 152–3. This point is a major theme of Rigg's last work, a study of Bunting.

75. J. H. Rigg, *Jabez Bunting, a Great Methodist Leader*, London: Kelly, 1905. In it, Rigg argues that, even in the 'Buntingite' era, more and more rights had been conceded to an increasingly educated laity, a process that had continued since, with such landmarks as the admission of laymen to the Conference in 1878.

76. Rigg, *View*, p. 171.

77. Currie, *Methodism Divided*, pp. 36, 52–3, for examples of 'bending' of rules.

78. Rigg, *Economy*, pp. 59–60, contrasts the vitality of Methodism, where 'in perfect accordance with the primitive and apostolic precedents, opportunity [is] afforded for the exercise of every gift of teaching possessed by the lay members of the church', with the failures, as he sees them, of 'independency' in this respect.

79. Currie, *Methodism Divided*, p. 79, for the view of the Reformers that local preachers and leaders were, effectively, co-pastors.

80. Gregory, *HCC*, p. 103. W. R. Ward (ed.), *The Early Correspondence of Jabez Bunting 1820–1829*, London: Royal Historical Society, 1972, pp. 108, 107.

81. Rigg, *View*, p. 222.

82. Rigg, *View*, pp. 222–3; Barrett, *Ministry*, pp. 24–5, 238.

83. Barrett, *Ministry*, p. 262.

84. Gregory, *HCC*, pp. 38–41.

85. Barrett, *Ministry*, p. 280.

86. Rigg, *View*, pp. 236–41.

87. Rigg, *View*, pp. 222–3.

88. Barrett, *Ministry*, p. 237; Rigg, *View*, pp. 55–70.

89. Shrewsbury, *Scriptural Character*, pp. 294–304.

90. Rigg, *Connexional Economy*, pp. 1–23; Gregory, *HCC*, p. 58.

91. Beck, 'Some Reflections on Connexionalism'.

92. Gregory, *HCC*, pp. 2–3, 213.

93. Gregory, *HCC*, p. 43.

94. For an interesting discussion of the struggle between 'conservatives' who wanted to keep to the compromise of 1878 and those 'liberals' who, in the 1890s, wanted more powers for the representative session of the Conference, see C. Oldstone-Moore, *Hugh Price Hughes*, Cardiff: University of Wales Press, 1999, pp. 257–9, 294–304.

95. E.g., Shrewsbury, *Scriptural Character*, p. 4.

96. See Butler, *Methodists and Papists*, and Rack, *Enthusiast*, pp. 305–13, for discussions of Wesley's complex attitude to Roman Catholicism. For this particular quotation, Wesley, *Works*, vol. 3, p. 52.

97. Cited in J. S. Simon, *A Summary of Methodist Law and Discipline*, London: Methodist Publishing House, 5th edn, revised to the Conference of 1923 by John Elsworth, 1924, pp. 268–9.

98. Shrewsbury, *Scriptural Character*, pp. 99–147.

99. Jackson, *Recollections*, pp. 450–7. In any case, Jackson, along with other Methodists, considered political agitation 'perilous to piety', p. 270.

100. J. H. Rigg, *Essays for the Times on ecclesiastical and social subjects*, London: Elliott Stock, 1866, p. 10.

101. For a representative Wesleyan view on questions of agitation for disestablishment and, indeed, political involvement on the part of ministers in general, see the anonymous, *Methodism in 1879* p. 89. For Rigg, see *Essays*, pp. 7, 82.

102. Gregory, HCC, pp. 7, 160, 166.

103. Gregory, HCC, pp. 176–9.

104. Gregory, HCC, p. 49.

105. Shrewsbury, *Scriptural Character*, pp. 88–9.

106. Shrewsbury, *Scriptural Character*, pp. 146–7.

107. Shrewsbury, *Scriptural Character*, p. 291.

108. Shrewsbury, *Scriptural Character*, p. 88.

109. Shrewsbury, *Scriptural Character*, pp. 321–44.

110. Shrewsbury, *Scriptural Character*, pp. 129–42.

111. Shrewsbury, *Scriptural Character*, p. 142.

112. Shrewsbury, *Scriptural Character*, pp. 142–3.

113. Barrett says little about unity in his main works, previously cited. However, in his *Pastoral Addresses: Adapted for Retirement and the Closet*, 2 vols, London: John Mason, 1849, vol. 2, there is an illuminating address, 'On the Unity of Believers in Christ', no. XXIV, pp. 369–84, which we examine briefly here.

114. Rigg, *View*, pp. 305–42.

115. Shrewsbury, *Scriptural Character*, p. 296.

116. Barrett, *Pastoral Addresses*, p. 371.

117. Barrett, *Pastoral Addresses*, pp. 380–1.

118. Gregory, HCC, pp. 152–3.

119. B. Gregory, *Sermons, Addresses and Pastoral Letters*, London, Wesleyan Conference Office, 1881, sermon on 'The Gathering Together of All Things in Christ', pp. 85–109, esp. pp. 86–8, 99–101.

120. Gregory, HCC, pp. 195–9.

121. Gregory, HCC, p. 204.

122. Rigg, *View*, pp. 332–3. *Proceedings of the Second Oecumenical Methodist Conference, 1891*, London: Charles H. Kelly, 1892, p. 109. Davies and Rupp (eds), *History*, vol. 4, pp. 587–8.

123. J. H. Rigg, *The Methodist Class Meeting*, London, 1865, p. 3.

124. Rigg, *View*, pp. 211, 213.

125. Gregory, HCC, p. 76.

126. Rigg, *Economy*, p. 185.

127. Rigg, *Economy*, pp. 192–3.

128. Rigg, *Economy*, p. 170. For an account of the changes made by Conference in 1889, see *Wesleyan Methodist Magazine* (1889), pp. 710–14.

129. J. S. Simon (1843–1933), a leading Wesleyan theologian and constitutional expert. See John Newton, 'Simon, Dr John Smith (1843–1933)', in

J. Vickers (ed.), *A Dictionary of Methodism in Britain and Ireland*, London: Epworth, 2000, p. 318. See Simon's *A Manual of Instruction and Advice for Class Leaders*, London: Methodist Publishing House, 1892, pp. 65–6.

130. S. W. Christophers, 'Class Meetings in their Relation to the Design of Methodism', *The Class Meeting in relation to the Discipline and Success of Methodism*, London: Wesleyan Methodist Book Room, 1873, ch. 1, pp. 1–32.

131. Rigg, *Economy*, pp. 1–23, 36–54.

132. Rigg, *Economy*, pp. 2–3.

133. Rigg, *View*, pp. 211–12.

134. Rigg, *View*, p. 248, and *Connexional Economy*, pp. 115–21.

135. Rigg, *Economy*, pp. 55–9; Gregory, *Handbook*, vol. 2, p. 271: 'in no other church is the mutual ministry of the people more recognised, guaranteed, insisted on and carried out, and in no other Church are the gifts of the individual members more utilised'.

136. Shrewsbury, *Scriptural Character*, pp. 225–49.

137. Rigg, *View*, p. 228.

138. Rigg, *View*, p. 235.

139. Rigg, *View*, pp. 236–41.

140. Rigg, *Economy*, pp. 71–2.

141. Shrewsbury, *Scriptural Character*, p. 298.

142. Rigg, *View*, pp. 28–36.

143. Rigg, *View*, p. 186.

144. On the Methodist New Connexion in general, the best introduction is still G. Packer (ed.), *The Centenary of the Methodist New Connexion*, London: G. Burroughs, 1897. On ecclesiology, see especially, the essays by: W. Longbottom, 'The Relation of the Methodist New Connexion to other Methodist Churches', pp. 179–229; T. Rider, 'The Spiritual Life and aims of the MNC', pp. 230–67; and W. J. Townsend, 'Church Principles and Order of the MNC', pp. 1–69.

145. Townsend, 'Church Principles', pp. 28, 43, 53.

146. Townsend, 'Church Principles', pp. 2, 4–5.

147. Rider, 'Spiritual Life', p. 265.

148. M. Baxter, *Methodism: Memorials of the United Methodist Free Churches*, London: W. Reed/Hamilton, Adams & Co., 1865, p. 285.

149. Kent, *Bunting*, gives a particularly clear account of the ecclesiological clash between Wesleyans and reformers. It is curious that the various groups of reformers never embraced pure congregationalism, with the supremacy of the 'church meeting' even though the logic of much of the scriptural exegesis adduced in support of their case would have pointed in that direction. Cf. Baxter, *Memorials* pp. 192–3, where he argues, in respect of several passages in Acts, that the whole people rather than purely the apostles or elders always had a determining say in appointments.

150. Cf. the arguments adduced by Daniel Isaac in *The Rules of the Protestant Methodists brought to the test of the Scriptures*, Leeds: Barr, 1830.

151. Baxter, *Methodism*, p. 243, refers to a dissident leaving Wesleyan Methodism in 1828, saying, 'I leave Methodism as it is, not as it was ... Methodism is under the influence of a priestly oligarchy ... it requires me to forgo not merely my civil rights as a Briton but my Scriptural rights as a Christian.'

152. Thus, Rigg argued that since the Church was effectively engaged in warfare against sin and unbelief, 'democratic' discipline was as inappropriate as it would be in the Army (*View*, pp. 170–1).

153. This point was often made obliquely rather than directly. Cf. the remarks of Hugh Bourne after being confronted with the choice between continuing his own methods of evangelism and submitting to Wesleyan discipline, 'I would be put out of the Methodist society and would be more use outside of it than within.' J. T. Wilkinson, *Hugh Bourne*, London: Epworth 1952, pp. 61–6, for details of his exclusion.

154. Cf. Bourne in Wilkinson, *Bourne*, p. 34, 'the desire for open-air worship was so implanted in me that nothing could shake it. In that respect, I was quite primitive.'

155. Thus, e.g., Bourne in 1812 cited Wesley speaking in 1790, 'Fellow labourers, wherever there is an open door, enter in and preach the Gospel ... go out quickly into the streets of the city and bring in the poor and maimed, the halt and lame ... this is the way the primitive Methodists did' (Wilkinson, *Bourne*, p. 92).

156. Kent, *Bunting*, p. 47.

157. W. H. Jones, *History of the Wesleyan Reform Union*, Epworth: London, 1952, p. 41.

158. Oliver Aveyard Beckerlegge, *The United Methodist Free Churches: A Study in Freedom*, London: Epworth, 1957, p. 67.

159. *A Short History of the Independent Methodists: A Souvenir of the Annual Meeting*, Warrington: Independent Methodist Book Room, 1905, p. 55. The Quaker influence on the Independent Methodists can be clearly seen in the following quotation from the same source: 'As Barclay the Quaker said, "Those who love the light must minister according to the light" ... All believers are in the ministry of service ... we set before the world a Church in which there are no distinctions of ministers and laity' (p. 58). Jones, *History*, p. 41.

3   Ecclesiology from Hughes to Flew

1. For Hughes, see both the classic biography by his daughter, Dorothea Hughes, *The Life of Hugh Price Hughes*, London: Hodder and Stoughton, 1904, and the modern scholarly biography by Oldstone-Moore, *Hughes*.

2. For Flew, see G. Wakefield, *Robert Newton Flew*, London: Epworth, 1969.

3. Hughes was responsible for the pioneering Grindelwald Conferences of 1892 that involved both Anglicans and free church people. Lidgett had a close relationship with Archbishop Davidson. Lidgett is dealt with in detail in a later section of this chapter.

4. G. K. A. Bell (ed.), *Documents on Christian Unity 1920–30*, 2 vols in 1, London: Oxford University Press, 2nd edn, 1930, pp. 108–10, for the reply of the Annual Conference of the Primitive Methodist Church (1926), and pp. 110–12, for the reply of the Annual Conference of the United Methodist Church (1926). 'An Appeal to all Christian people' was issued by the Lambeth Conference of 1920, inviting them to work towards the reunion of Christendom on the basis of an acceptance of the Holy Scriptures, the Nicene and Apostles' Creeds, the two sacraments of Baptism and Holy Communion, and a ministry acceptable to the whole Church (Bell, *Documents*, pp. 1–5, for full text of the appeal).

5. The controversy over the writings of Agar Beet from 1897 to 1905 was a defining epoch for Wesleyan Methodism. See D. Carter, 'Joseph Agar Beet and the Eschatological Crisis', *Proceedings of the Wesley Historical Society*, 51, 6, (1998), pp. 197–216.

6. The contributions of Hughes and Scott Lidgett are referred to in later sections of this chapter.

7. A. W. Harrison, 'Methodist Churchmanship', *London and Holborn Quarterly Review* (1938), pp. 193–6 (195).

8. On the one hand, Methodist leaders came increasingly round to the view that the 'coming great church' would include episcopal, presbyterian and congregational elements. Despite the reservations of some, they allowed Methodists in South India to press ahead with the scheme for union there that from almost the first envisaged an episcopally led church. On the other hand, the statement of W. F. Lofthouse, 'The Possibility of a United Christendom from the Standpoint of Methodism', in K. MacKenzie (ed.), *Union of Christendom*, London: SPCK, 1938, pp. 479–502 (493), that 'the Methodist is not greatly concerned with continuity or tradition' shows that few Methodists as yet were engaging really seriously with issues that were so important to much of the rest of Christendom.

9. H. M. Hughes, *Christian Foundations*, London: Epworth, 1927, p. 166.

10. For the United Methodist Free Churches, see Beckerlegge, *United Methodist Free Churches*.

11. Rigg, *View*, deals copiously with this issue in pp. 307–34.

12. See the recent study by Martin Wellings, 'Making Haste Slowly: The Campaign for Lay Representation in the Wesleyan Conference 1871–8', *Proceedings of the Wesley Historical Society*, 53, 2 (2001), pp. 25–37.

13. Longbottom, 'Relation of the Methodist New Connexion'.

14. Statement of the Conferences of 1908 and 1913 to accompany the Rules of the Society, cited in Simon (ed.), *Summary*, pp. 9–14.

15. Davies, George and Rupp (eds), *History*, vol. 3, pp. 324–8.

16. Davies, George and Rupp (eds), *History*, vol. 3, p. 333.

17. G. Eayrs, *British Methodism, as It Is, as It Was, as It Will Be: A Popular Handbook and History to Help Methodist Union*, London: Henry Hooks, 1909, esp. pp. 4–6, 9, 38–44. George Eayrs (1864–1926) was a United Methodist minister.

18. Perks is cited directly in Eayrs, *British Methodism*, pp. 4–6.

19. Eayrs, *British Methodism*, esp. pp. 13, 23, 27, 31–3.

20. A. J. Bolton, *The Other Side*, Peterborough: WMHS Publications, 1994.

21. Davies, George and Rupp (eds), *History*, vol. 3, p. 337.

22. The lay Vice-Presidency was a United and Primitive Methodist demand. Currie, *Methodism Divided*, p. 255.

23. 'Deed of Union', in *The Constitutional Practice and Discipline of the Methodist Church*, Peterborough: Methodist Publishing House, 1999, vol. 2, pp. 212–14.

24. Wesley, *Works*, vol. 1, p. 129.

25. Cf. *Statements and Reports of the Methodist Church on Faith and Order*, vol. 1, *1933–83*, Peterborough: Methodist Publishing House, 1984, pp. 124–45.

26. Contrast the statement of the Deed of Union with the remark by Lofthouse, 'Possibility of a United Christendom', p. 486, 'Membership of the Church is not constituted by baptism, or by participating in the Eucharist, or indeed by accepting any form of creed save faith in Jesus as the divine Saviour. Neither baptism nor participation in the Eucharist is set down as necessary for membership, although it is expected (not required) that every member will be baptised, and every member is exhorted to attend the communion with regularity.'

27. G. G. Findlay, *The Church of Christ as set forth in the New Testament*, London: Kelly, 1893, p. 75.

28. Findlay, *Church*, p. 37.

29. Findlay, *Church*, pp. 20, 36.

30. G. G. Findlay, *The Epistle to the Ephesians*, London: Hodder and Stoughton, 1888, pp. 143–4.

31. Cited in L. Thunberg, *Man and the Cosmos*, New York: St Vladimir's Press, 1985, p. 75.

32. Findlay, *Ephesians*, pp. 206–9.

33. Findlay, *Ephesians*, pp. 93–4.

34. Findlay, *Ephesians*, pp. 367–8.

35. Findlay, *Ephesians*, pp. 257, 223.

36. Findlay, *Ephesians*, p. 9. See also Jean-Marie Tillard, 'Faith, the Believer and the Church', *One in Christ*, 30, 3 (1994), pp. 216–28.

37. Findlay, *Ephesians*, p. 193.

38. Findlay, *Ephesians*, pp. 201, 206, 208–9.

39. Statement of the Nottingham Conference in the 'Not Strangers but Pilgrims Process', 1987, para. 2.

40. Oldstone-Moore, *Hughes*, p. 156.

41. Oldstone-Moore, *Hughes*, pp. 135–8.

42. D. Hughes, *Hughes*, pp. 435–80; Oldstone-Moore, *Hughes*, pp. 156–7, 230–1.

43. Oldstone-Moore, *Hughes*, pp. 228–38, 272–80. Hughes was well ahead of many of his time in emphasizing the importance of corporate reunion. 'However much churches might fraternise and co-operate, they would never succeed until they united' (p. 236). He also championed episcopacy on grounds both of effectiveness in mission and antiquity (p. 233). His boldness in this astonished many Anglicans as well as Methodists.

44. Oldstone-Moore, *Hughes*, p. 243.

45. Oldstone-Moore, *Hughes*, p. 221.

46. D. Hughes, *Hughes*, p. 448.

47. Oldstone-Moore, *Hughes*, p. 2.

48. Oldstone-Moore, *Hughes*, p. 230.

49. Oldstone-Moore, *Hughes*, pp. 228, 233.

50. Oldstone-Moore, *Hughes*, pp. 80–1.

51. D. Hughes, *Hughes*, p. 440.

52. D. Hughes, *Hughes*, pp. 394–5.

53. Oldstone-Moore, *Hughes*, pp. 299–300.

54. There is no major biography of Beet. A brief obituary appeared in the *Wesleyan Methodist Magazine*, May 1924. My article on Beet (see n. 5 above, for full details) contains a little further biographical background.

55. A MS notebook containing some of Beet's lectures in church history is preserved in the John Rylands Library, Manchester.

56. J. A. Beet, *The Church and the Sacraments*, London: Hodder and Stoughton, 1907.

57. Beet, *Church*, pp. 16–17.

58. Beet, *Church*, pp. 20–3.

59. Beet, *Church*, p. 154.

60. Beet, *Church*, pp. 68ff.

61. Beet, MSS.

62. Rigg, *Connexional Economy*, p. 192.

63. Beet, *Church*, pp. 85–6.

64. J. A. Beet, *A Manual of Theology*, London: Hodder and Stoughton, 1907, p. 387.

65. Beet, *Church*, p. 90.

66. Beet, *Church*, pp. 89–90; also Beet, *Manual*, pp. 386–7.

67. M. Thurian, *The Eucharistic Memorial* (ET), London: Lutterworth, 1961.

68. Beet, *Church*, p. 68.

69. Beet, *Church*, pp. 80–1.

70. John Paul II, *Ut Unum Sint*, London: Catholic Truth Society, 1995, para. 85.

71. The best overall study of Lidgett's career is R.E. Davies (ed.), *John Scott Lidgett: A Symposium*, London: Epworth, 1957. See also Alan Turberfield's Oxford D. Phil. thesis 'A Critical Appraisal of John Scott Lidgett', 1998, p. 368. Epworth Press anticipates publishing in 2003 a biography of Scott Lidgett by Alan Turberfield.

72. Davies, *Lidgett*, pp. 79–106 and 183–210, for assessments of Lidgett as theologian and ecumenical statesman.

73. J. S. Lidgett, *God, Christ and the Church* London: Hodder and Stoughton, 1927, p. 223.

74. J. S. Lidgett, *God in Christ Jesus*, London: Epworth, 1915, commentary on Ephesians, pp. 220–3, for this amplification.

75. Lidgett, *God in Christ Jesus*, p. 247.

76. Gregory, *HCC*, p. 18; Zizioulas, *Being as Communion*; Lidgett, *God in Christ Jesus*, p. 249.

77. Lidgett, *God in Christ Jesus*, p. 260; cf. also *The Apostolic Ministry: Sermons and Addresses*, London: Robert Culley, 1910, p. 124.

78. Lidgett, *God in Christ Jesus*, p. 264.

79. Lidgett, *God in Christ Jesus*, pp. 264–5.

80. Lidgett, *God in Christ Jesus*, p. 265.

81. Lidgett, *God, Christ and the Church*, p. 262.

82. Lidgett, *Apostolic Ministry*, pp. 106–29. See esp. pp. 109–11, 118–19 and 128. Lidgett, *God in Christ Jesus*, pp. 273–89.

83. Lidgett, *God, Christ and the Church*, p. 277.

84. Lidgett *God, Christ and the Church*, p. 231.

85. Lidgett began his *Fatherhood of God*, Edinburgh: T. & T. Clark, 1902, with a repudiation of any such sentimentality, p. 4.

86. Lidgett, *God, Christ and the Church*, pp. 279–80.

87. Lidgett, *God, Christ and the Church*, pp. 229–30.

88. Lidgett, *God, Christ and the Church*, p. 240.

89. Lidgett, *God, Christ and the Church*, pp. 226–7.

90. G. Tavard, 'Tradition as Koinonia', *One in Christ*, 24, 2 (1988), pp. 97–111 (110).

91. Lidgett, *God, Christ and the Church*, p. 221.

92. Lidgett, *God, Christ and the Church*, p. 235.

93. Lidgett, *God, Christ and the Church*, pp. 235–6.

94. Lidgett, *God, Christ and the Church*, pp. 292–300.
95. Lidgett, *God, Christ and the Church*, pp. 310–20.
96. Lidgett, *God, Christ and the Church*, p. 320.
97. H. Bett, *Spirit of Methodism*, London: Epworth, 1937, pp. 144–5.
98. Lidgett, *God, Christ and the Church*, p. 245.
99. Lidgett, *God, Christ and the Church*, pp. 265–8.
100. Lidgett, *God, Christ and the Church*, pp. 229–30, 256.
101. Lidgett, *God, Christ and the Church*, p. 231.
102. See, e.g., the reference above (n. 4) to the response of the United Methodist Conference to the 'Lambeth Appeal', and *Statements*, vol. 1 p. 206. Note also Lidgett's emphasis in *God, Christ and the Church*, p. 262, upon the need for a 'common order and a common ministry . . . that must be universally recognised'.
103. G. Wainwright (1939–) now teaches at Duke University in the USA. He masterminded the 'Baptism, Eucharist, Ministry' Process of the World Council of Churches and has been involved in five of Methodism's international dialogues with other Christian traditions. Two of his books, *The Ecumenical Moment: Crisis and Opportunity for the Church*, Grand Rapids: Eerdmans, 1983, and *Methodists in Dialog*, Nashville: Kingswood, 1995, give ample testimony to his work. He has also written a biography of the ecumenical pioneer, Lesslie Newbigin.
104. The standard biography of Peake is John T. Wilkinson, *Arthur Samuel Peake: A Biography*, London: Epworth, 1971.
105. Wilkinson, *Peake*, ch. 9, 'The Ecumenical Churchman', pp. 156–72, and esp. pp. 156–7, 158–9, 163–4.
106. G. Thompson Brake, *Policy and Politics in British Methodism, 1932–82*, London: Edsall, 1984, pp. 341–2.
107. Brake, *Policy*, p. 342.
108. R. N. Flew, *Jesus and His Church*, London: Epworth, 1938.
109. Flew, *Jesus*, pp. 35–88.
110. *Statements*, vol. 1, pp. 7, 16, 22, 40–1.
111. *Statements*, vol. 1, pp. 15, 16.
112. *Statements*, vol. 1, p. 11.
113. Flew, *Jesus*, p. 182.
114. *Statements*, vol. 1, p. 7.
115. *Statements*, vol. 1, pp. 22–3.
116. *Statements*, vol. 1, p. 12.
117. *Statements*, vol. 1, pp. 10–11.
118. *Statements*, vol. 1, p. 9.
119. *Statements*, vol. 1, p. 15.
120. Flew, *Jesus*, p. 111.
121. *Statements*, vol. 1, p. 28; cf. Gregory, *HCC*, p. 7.
122. *Statements*, vol. 1, pp. 31–2.

123. For the modern ecumenical consensus on apostolicity as a bundle of characteristics, see para. M34 of the 'Baptism, Eucharist, Ministry' statement of the Faith and Order Commission of the World Council of Churches. The architects of the 1937 statement were concerned to repudiate the idea that apostolicity alone resided in the possession of the 'three fold ministry', transmitted in unbroken succession from the apostles. See *Statements*, vol. 1, p. 26.

124. *Statements*, vol. 1, pp. 23–8, esp. p. 27.

125. *Statements*, vol. 1, pp. 33–6. For Findlay, see pp. 77–81.

126. *Statements*, vol. 1, pp. 37–9.

127. *Statements*, vol. 1, p. 41.

4   Called to Love and Praise

1. These statements are listed in *Statements*, vol. 1. Those on ordination are at pp. 124–49. The significance of these will be more fully explored in the next chapter.

2. Kissack, *Church*, esp. pp. 137–59, for the points alluded to above. The BEM process itself raised many ecclesiological questions. See *Baptism, Eucharist and Ministry: Report on the Process and Responses*, Faith and Order Paper, 149, Geneva: World Council of Churches, 1990.

3. The assumption that there was one biblical theology underlay such great works as Kittel's famous *Worterbuch zum neuen Testament* (ET: Gerhard Kittel and Gerhard Friedrich (eds), *Theological Dictionary of the New Testament*, trans. Geoffrey W. Bromiley, 10 vols, Grand Rapids: Eerdmans, 1964–).

4. The immense variety of traditions within the New Testament was demonstrated most comprehensively by J. P. G. Dunn, *Unity and Diversity in the New Testament*, London: SCM Press, 1977. For particular consideration of ecclesiology and ministry, see also E. Schweizer, *Church Order in the New Testament* (ET), London: SCM Press, 1959.

5. *Called To Love and Praise: A Methodist Conference Statement on the Church*, Peterborough: Methodist Publishing House, 1999 (*CLP*), paras 1.2.5–1.2.9. (Note that all referencing of this document is by paragraph, except where explicitly done by section.)

6. *CLP*, 1.1.1.

7. *CLP*, 1.2.5.

8. *CLP*, 1.2.6–1.2.7.

9. The dialogues include the 'Baptism, Ministry, Eucharist' Process of the World Council of Churches; also dialogues with the Roman Catholic Church, the Anglican Communion, the Lutheran World Federation, the World Alliance of Reformed Churches and a preliminary dialogue with the Orthodox. The details of most of these can be found in H. Meyer and

L. Vischer (eds), *Growth in Agreement: Reports and Agreed Statements of Ecumenical Conversations on a World Level*, Geneva: World Council of Churches/New York: Paulist, 1984, and in J. Gros, H. Meyer and W. Rusch (eds), *Growth in Agreement II: Reports and Agreed Statements of Ecumenical Conversations on a World Level, 1982–1998*, Geneva: World Council of Churches/Grand Rapids: Eerdmans, 2000. For local ecumenical partnerships, see R. Nunn, *This Growing Unity*, London: Churches Together in England, 1995.

10. For the four noted, *CLP*, section 2.4; Methodism, section 4.

11. 'Nature of the Christian Church' (NCC), in *Statements*, vol. 1, pp. 30–3, 37–9.

12. *CLP*, 1.2.9.

13. By the 'Wesleyan Quadrilateral', Albert Outler and others meant the interplay within the Wesleyan theological tradition of Scripture, Tradition, reason and experience; for the Montreal Statement, see M. Kinnamon and B. Cope (eds), *The Ecumenical Movement: An Anthology of Texts*, Geneva: WCC, 1997, pp. 139–44; for Vatican II, see Decree *Dei Verbum*, cited in W. M. Abbott (ed.), *Documents of Vatican II*, London: Geoffrey Chapman, 1966, pp. 111–28.

14. *CLP*, 1.2.10.

15. The question of teaching authority is not really discussed. The most recent quinquennium (1997–2001) of the Roman Catholic–Methodist dialogue dealt with this issue. Its findings, briefly discussed in the final chapter, will be important for future Methodist work on the question.

16. *CLP*, 1.3.1–1.3.3.

17. *CLP*, 1.4.3, and section 2.1.

18. See, e.g., L. Davison, *Sender and Sent: A Study in Mission*, London: Epworth, 1969. T. F. Best and G. Gassmann (eds), *On the Way to Fuller Koinonia*, Faith and Order Paper 166, Geneva: WCC, 1994.

19. *CLP*, 1.4.2, and section 2.2.

20. *CLP*, section 2.3.

21. *CLP*, section 2.4.

22. *CLP*, section 5.5.

23. *CLP*, 1.4.3; section 2.1, esp. 2.1.9.

24. *CLP*, 2.1.1, 2.1.6.

25. *CLP*, 2.1.8.

26. *CLP*, 2.1.7.

27. *CLP*, 2.1.10.

28. *CLP*, 2.1.9.

29. *The Apostolic Tradition*, para. 13, cited in Gros, Meyer and Rusch (eds), *Growth II*, p. 600.

30. D. H. Tripp, *The Renewal of the Covenant in the Methodist Tradition*, London: Epworth, 1969.*CLP*, 2.2.1–2.2.9.

31. CLP, 2.2.8–2.2.10.
32. See above, n. 4.
33. CLP, 2.3.1, 2.3.3.
34. CLP, 2.3.4–2.3.6.
35. CLP, 2.3.8.
36. CLP, 2.3.18.
37. CLP, 2.4.3.
38. CLP, 2.4.2.
39. CLP, 2.4.3.
40. CLP, 2.4.4.
41. CLP, 2.4.7; Gregory, *HCC*, p. 154.
42. CLP, 2.4.6.
43. CLP, 2.4.8–2.4.9.
44. CLP, 2.4.10.
45. Gregory, *HCC*, p. 6.
46. CLP, 2.4.10.
47. CLP, 2.4.12–2.4.13. Cf. Kissack, *Church*, p. 145.
48. CLP, 3.1.13.
49. Particularly in respect of the different branches of Methodism. Rigg, *View*, p. 334.
50. CLP, 3.1.1.
51. Cf. the declarations made by Conference in response to the world conferences on faith and order. *Statements*, vol. 1, pp. 238–44.
52. Details in response submitted from Conference Office to the 'Called to Be One' Process.
53. CLP, 3.1.1.
54. CLP, 3.1.7.
55. CLP, 3.1.8.
56. CLP, 3.1.1, 13.1.16, 13.1.17.
57. Quick, *Methodism*, throughout.
58. CLP, 3.1.18. Conversations involving closer relations are being held at the time of writing with Anglicans in England, Scotland and Wales; there are 'informal' conversations' in England also involving the URC as well; in Wales there are separate talks about the feasibility of a united free church.
59. CLP, 3.2.2.
60. CLP, 3.2.4.
61. CLP, 3.2.11.
62. CLP, 3.2.13.
63. CLP, 3.2.15.
64. CLP, 3.2.16.
65. CLP, 4.1, 4.2.14.
66. T. Macquiban, with additional comment by Rupert Hoare, Michael

Townsend and Reg Ward, 'Does Methodism Matter Enough?', *Epworth Review*, 23, 2 (1996), pp. 67–80.

67. Revd Dr M. Wilshaw, former Chair, London SE District.

68. *CLP*, section 4.6.

69. *CLP*, section 4.2.

70. Terms like 'fellowship group' etc. are sometimes used in place of the original 'class meeting' but this should not blind us to the fact that there is still a widespread sense that this is a proper part of Methodist belonging, even though the disciplinary function is now effectively dead and no one now seriously suggests that attendance in class should still be compulsory.

71. The strong stress on nurturing in the 1936 *Book of Offices* baptismal service probably contributed to this: pp. 97–104 for service of baptism of infants, esp. pp. 99–100.

72. A further reference to this is made in *CLP*, 4.4.5.

73. *Methodist Service Book*, London: Methodist Publishing House, 1975, pp. A14–26.

74. See, e.g., the report on *Baptism and Church Membership, with particular reference to Local Ecumenical Partnerships*, by a Churches Together in England working party, London: CTE, 1997.

75. *CLP*, 4.4.3–4.4.4.

76. *CLP*, 4.4.5.

77. *CLP*, 4.4.8.

78. *CLP*, 4.4.13.

79. As presented to the 1999 Conference. *Agenda*, pp. 324–71. The 'assessment' is the levy requested from local churches for their share of circuit, district and connexional expenses. Traditionally, it has been estimated according to the 'membership' of each local society. This is now frequently felt to be unsatisfactory, failing to take account of any non-members, who may yet be regular attenders at a local church or of the relative wealth or poverty of the community.

80. *CLP*, section 4.5.

81. For examples, see last section of ch. 2 (pp. 63–7).

82. For an example of the sort of points raised, see correspondence in *Methodist Recorder*, 6–20 April 2000.

83. Wesleyan 'probationer' ministers had been authorized to preside at the Eucharist. Whether they should, before their ordination and 'reception into full connexion', be regarded as lay is a moot point, though the Wesleyan tradition had been to style them the 'Reverend' from their entry into circuit, a privilege which distinguished them from the laity even though they had not yet received the final and solemn ratification of their ministerial status.

Wesley had distinguished between the 'covenanted' means of grace, prescribed in Scripture, and the 'prudential'. The former were both sacra-

mental and non-sacramental, including prayer, attendance at public worship and reading of Scripture. The last included later Methodist devotional
practices, e.g., meeting in class.

84. *CLP*, 4.5.2.

85. *CLP*, 4.5.3.

86. *CLP*, 4.5.3.

87. *CLP*, 4.5.4. See also *Statements and Reports of the Methodist
Church on Faith and Order*, vol. 2, Peterborough: Methodist Publishing
House, 2000, pp. 229–81.

88. *Statements*, vol. 2, pp. 229–81, citing report *Ministry of the People
of God*.

89. *CLP*, 4.5.5–4.5.14.

90. *CLP*, 4.5.11.

91. *CLP*, 4.5.10; *Statements*, vol. 1, pp. 132–48.

92. See, e.g., H. R. McAdoo and Alan Clark (eds), *The Final Report*,
London: Catholic Truth Society/SPCK, 1982, p. 36: 'nevertheless their
ministry is not an extension of the common Christian priesthood, but
belongs to another realm of the gifts of the Spirit'. See also Meyer and
Vischer (eds), *Growth*, pp. 61–130.

93. NCC in *Statements*, vol. 1, p. 27.

94. I have explored the possibility of a reconciliation of some traditionally Wesleyan insights into the 'pastoral office' with those of the 'catholic'
tradition in D. Carter, 'Pastoral Office or Sacrificing Priesthood: Towards
Reconciliation in Concepts of Presbyteral/Episcopal Ministry', *Methodist
Sacramental Fellowship Bulletin*, 127, (1998), pp. 31–47.

95. A point made by Brian Beck in his article 'Some Reflections on
Connexionalism', *Epworth Review*, 18, 2/3, (1991), 2, p. 57, 3 pp. 49–50,
for this specific point.

96. *CLP*, section 4.6.

97. See, esp. Rigg, *Economy*, chs 4 and 8.

98. See Eayrs, *British Methodism*, cited in ch. 3.

99. B. Beck, 'Some Reflections on Connexionalism'.

100. Tavard, 'Dialogue', p. 180.

101. *CLP*, 4.6.1, 4.6.3, 4.6.5.

102. *CLP*, 4.6.3.

103. *CLP*, 4.6.8.

104. *CLP*, 4.6.1, 4.6.9, 4.6.11.

105. *Statements*, vol. 1, pp. 232–7.

106. *CLP*, 4.6.10.

107. *CLP*, 4.6.11.

108. *Statements*, vol. 2, pp. 383–411.

109. *CLP*, 4.6.1. See also D. Carter, 'A Methodist Reaction to *Ut
Unum Sint*', *One in Christ*, 33, 2 (1997), pp. 125–37.

110. *CLP*, 4.6.6.

111. *CLP*, 4.6.2, 4.6.3.

112. For an account of the US system, see Frank, *Polity*. See also Robbins and Carter, 'Connexionalism and Koinonia'.

113. *CLP*, 4.7.8.

114. *CLP*, 4.7.4–4.7.7.

115. *CLP*, 4.7.7.

116. Bishop William Boyd Grove, the Ecumenical Officer of the United Methodist Council of Bishops, was a UM representative at the 1999 Conference and showed great enthusiasm for the report.

5 The Methodist Doctrine of Ministry

1. See chs 1 and 2 for developments under Wesley and the changes in the nineteenth century. For the Roman Catholic–Methodist dialogue, see 'Apostolic Tradition', paras 70–98, in Gros, Meyer and Rusch (eds), *Growth II*, pp. 612–16.

2. NCC, pp. 23–7, cited in 'Ordination in the Methodist Church', 1960, cited in *Statements*, vol. 1, pp. 124–5.

3. Cited in Document 61, in B. Tabraham (ed.), *Documents, Methodism and Wesley Studies*, London: Methodist Open Learning Centre, no date given; source cited as Dr Bunting's Visit to Leeds, 19 June 1850, Leeds, 1850, pp. 25–6.

4. Gregory, *Handbook*, vol. 2, p. 25. For comparison of stewards with diaconate, see 'Ordination, 1974', in *Statements*, vol. 1, p. 144.

5. See, e.g., the British Methodist Lima response. M. Thurian (ed.), *Churches Respond to BEM*, 6 vols, Geneva: WCC, 1986, vol. 2, p. 215.

6. For a particularly notable example of this, see the discussions on episcopacy below and in the material on episcopacy from 1978 to 1982, in *Statements*, vol. 1, pp. 202–37.

7. For a short survey of changes in the ministry from the 1960s, see J. M. Turner, *Modern Methodism in England 1932–1998*, London: Epworth, 1998, pp. 24–5. For a more detailed survey of the genesis and development of changes in the sixties and seventies of the twentieth century, see Brake, *Policy and Politics in British Methodism 1932–82*, pp. 289–339; for sector ministry, see especially pp. 299–301, 302–5, 309–10; for 'recognized and regarded' ministers, see p. 372.

8. And, indeed, was faithfully attended to by the Faith and Order Committee. Both the reports on the diaconate and those on the possible adoption of episcopacy paid close attention to ecumenical models and understanding.

9. *Statements*, vol. 1, pp. 124–49, 202–37; also *Statements and Reports of the Methodist Church on Faith and Order*, vol. 2, 1984–2000, Peter-

borough: Methodist Publishing House, 2000, pt 1, pp. 195–281 and 291–346.

10. *Statements*, vol. 1, p. 124.

11. *Statements*, vol. 1, p. 129, where it is recorded that the standing vote of the Conference is integral to making a minister and that no person ordaining does so purely on their own authority and without that of the Conference.

12. *Statements*, vol. 1, p. 126.

13. *Statements*, vol. 1, p. 134.

14. *Statements*, vol. 1, p. 136.

15. Gregory, *HCC*, p. 103. For the modern ecumenical theology of *koinonia* and its implications for the understanding of ministry, see Best and Gassmann (eds), *On the Way to Fuller Koinonia*, pp. 284–5; also the ARCIC report on *koinonia* in Gros, Meyer and Rusch (eds), *Growth II*, pp. 328–43.

16. 1960 report, in *Statements*, vol. 1, pp. 128–30; 1974 report, in *Statements*, vol. 1, pp. 137–8.

17. *Baptism, Eucharist, Ministry* [*Lima*], Geneva: World Council of Churches, 1982, para. M34, cited in Kinnamon (ed.), *Anthology*, p. 196; see also the recent Porvoo Agreement between British and Irish Anglicans and Baltic and Scandinavian Lutheran churches, where the expression 'sign but not guarantee' is used.

18. See, e.g., Barrett, *Ministry*, pp. 282–3, 338.

19. J.-M. Tillard, *L'eglise locale*, Paris: Editions du Cerf, 1995, pp. 219–49.

20. *Statements*, vol. 1, pp. 144–6. One can validly question how far the functions of Methodist stewards ever have really corresponded with those of the 'Reformation' concept of 'diaconos'. As the later Faith and Order statement of 1993 shows, the 'Reformation' deacon in Geneva was concerned with the poor; only the 'poor' stewards in Methodism, as opposed to other stewards, had any real connection with this function.

21. *Statements*, vol. 1, pp. 145–6.

22. *Statements*, vol. 2, p. 291.

23. *Statements*, vol 2, p. 308.

24. *Statements*, vol. 1, pp. 202–36. For specific discussion of who might become bishops, see pp. 215–20.

25. *Statements*, vol. 1, p. 206.

26. *Statements*, vol. 1, p. 206. It should, however, be noted that two members of the working party signed a dissentient report, pp. 226–7, arguing that 'we cannot believe that the acceptance of the historic episcopate into the Methodist Church would serve any useful purpose'. Another member said that she could only accept the proposals provided there was mutual acceptance of ministries.

27. *Statements*, vol. 1, pp. 209–12.

28. *Statements*, vol. 1, p. 212.
29. *Statements*, vol. 1, pp. 213–14.
30. See, e.g. the work of Jean-Marie Tillard in the Roman Catholic tradition, with his constant emphasis upon the 'bishop' listening to and safeguarding the traditions of his local church as well as representing the concerns of the wider church to the local church. Tillard, *L' Eglise Locale*, throughout; also the recent Church of England House of Bishops' Report on *Bishops in Communion: Collegiality in the Service of the Koinonia of the Church*, London: Church House Publishing, 2000.
31. *Statements*, vol. 1, pp. 215–19.
32. *Statements*, vol. 2, pp. 195–281.
33. *Statements*, vol. 2, p. 198.
34. *Statements*, vol. 2, p. 201.
35. *Statements*, vol. 2, p. 210. *Lima*, para. M26, in Kinnamon (ed.), *Anthology*, p. 196.
36. *Statements*, vol. 2, pp. 263–6, for the careful discussion of this.

Summary, Conclusions, Prospects

1. *CLP*, 5.4.
2. *Statements*, vol. 2, pp. 383–411.
3. *CLP*, 2.4.6, for the reference to the 'sign of the episcopal succession'. Section 4.5 of *CLP* is concerned with the relationship of the ministry to the priesthood of all believers and says very little about *episkope*.
4. *Statements*, vol. 2, pp. 385–7.
5. *BEM*, paras M26–9.
6. *Statements*, vol. 2, pp. 389–90.
7. *Statements*, vol. 2, pp. 389–90, 391–2. The 'Connexional Team' consists of national officers responsible for coordinating the Connexion and giving advice on various activities. Thus, for example, it includes the Local Preachers' Secretary, responsible for the initial and ongoing training of local preachers. The various officers of the Connexional Team are appointed by the Conference and work under its ultimate direction. Four 'coordinating' secretaries exercise a degree of supervision over sub-teams within the Connexional Team.
8. *Methodist Recorder*, 13 September 2001.
9. *Statements*, vol. 2, pp. 394–407.
10. *Statements*, vol. 2, pp. 407–9.
11. *Statements*, vol. 2, p. 409.
12. *Statements*, vol. 2, p. 404.
13. In Scotland the SCIFU (Scottish Churches' Initiative for Union) scheme envisages an episcopal church. In Wales there is a plan for an 'ecumenical bishop' in East Cardiff. There are also discussions involving

the Anglican and Methodist churches across Wales as well as the scheme for a United Free Church in Wales.

14. See the interim report of the Formal Conversations, *Commitment to Mission and Unity*, London: Church House Publishing/Peterborough: Methodist Publishing House, 1996.

15. *Speaking the Truth in Love: Teaching Authority among Catholics and Methodists*, report of the Joint Commission for Dialogue between the Roman Catholic Church and the World Methodist Council, Lake Junaluska: World Methodist Council, 2001. I understand this report will be made available from the Methodist Publishing House.

16. *Speaking*, para. 120.

17. Held at Wesley House, Cambridge, in September 2001. The papers will be published in June 2002 by Epworth Press under the title *What Is a Minister?*, edited by P. Luscombe and E. Shreeve.

18. *An Anglican–Methodist Covenant: Common Statement of the Formal Conversations between the Methodist Church of Great Britain and the Church of England*, Peterborough: Methodist Publishing House: London/ Church House Publishing, 2001, pp 60–1.

19. For the texts of these statements, see *On the Way to Visible Unity: The Meissen Common Statement, 1988*, London: Board of Mission and Unity, Church House Publishing, 1988, esp. pp. 17–18. *Called to Witness and Service: The Reuilly Common Statement*, London: Church House Publishing, 1999, pp. 13–40, esp. the 'Joint Declaration' on pp. 36–8.

20. E.g. *Covenant*, p. 43, para. 134, for differences within the two churches on the Eucharist.

21. *HP* 756.

22. E.g. *HP* 812, Gregory, *HCC*, p. 213.

23. *Conversations on the Way to Unity: The Report of the Informal Conversations between the Church Of England, the Methodist Church and the United Reformed Church*, London: United Reformed Church, 2001, pp. 11, 19.

24. Frank, *Polity*, gives a full account of US global connexionalism.

25. See, e.g., the work of the French Catholic ecclesiologist, Jean Rigal, *L'ecclesiologie de communion*, Paris: Editions du Cerf, 1997.

26. Lawson, *Ministry*, p. 75, citing a discussion at the Conference of 1747.

27. Gregory, *HCC*, p. 7.

28. Jackson, *Wesleyan Methodism*; *NCC*, p. 33. Slater and Quick: see n. 30.

29. *BEM*, para. M34.

30. W. F. Slater, *Methodism in the Light of the Early Church*, London: T. Woolmer, 1885; W. A. Quick, *Methodism, a Parallel*, London: T. Woolmer, 1889.

31. For these agreements, see, respectively, *Together in Mission and Ministry*, London: Church House Publishing, 1993, pp. 1–33; *On the Way to Visible Unity*, pp. 7–32; and *Called to Witness and Service*, pp. 5–43.

32. See especially in this context the work of the French ecumenical Groupe des Dombes, much of the gist of which is summarized in the work of one of the Roman Catholic participants, Père B. Sesboue. See his *Pour une theologie oecumenique*, Paris: Editions du Cerf, 1990, pp. 287–312.

33. 'Towards a Statement on the Church', para. 58, cited in Gros, Meyer and Rusch (eds), *Growth II*, p. 593.

34. Shrewsbury, *Scriptural Character*, pp. 146–7, 88.

35. Gregory, *HCC*, p. 54. J. A. Mohler, *De l'unité de l'église ou du principe du catholicisme*, Brussels, 1839, p. 163.

36. Wesley, *Works*, vol. 2, sermon 39, pp. 81–95; Brake, *Policy*, p. 829; CLP, 2.4.4.

37. *Covenant*, p. 60.

Bibliography

General works on Methodism and the Wesleys

Davies , R. E., *Methodism*, London: Penguin, 1963.

Davies R. E., A. R. George and G. Rupp, *A History of the Methodist Church in Great Britain*, 4 vols, London: Epworth, 1965–88.

Frank, Thomas E., *Polity, Practice and Mission of the United Methodist Church*, Nashville: Abingdon, 1997.

Heitzenrater, R., *Wesley and the People Called Methodists*, Nashville: Abingdon, 1995.

Hymns and Psalms, London: Methodist Publishing House, 1983.

Jackson, T. (ed.), *Works of Rev. John Wesley*, London: John Mason, 1856.

Jones, W. H., *History of the Wesleyan Reform Union*, Epworth: London, 1952.

Maddox, R., *Responsible Grace: John Wesley's Practical Theology*, Nashville: Abingdon, 1994.

The Methodist Hymn Book, London: Methodist Publishing House, 1904 and 1933 edns.

Osborne, G. (ed.), *Poetical Works of John and Charles Wesley*, 12 vols, London: Wesleyan Conference Office, 1868.

Rack, H., *The Future of John Wesley's Methodism*, London: Lutterworth, 1965.

Rack, H., *Reasonable Enthusiast: John Wesley and the Rise of Methodism*, London: Epworth, 1989

Runyon, T., *The New Creation: John Wesley's Theology Today*, Nashville: Abingdon, 1998.

A Short History of the Independent Methodists: A Souvenir of the Annual Meeting, Warrington: Independent Methodist Book Room, 1905.

Tabraham, B. (ed.), *Documents, Methodism and Wesley Studies*, London: Methodist Open Learning Centre, n.d.

Telford, J. (ed.), *Letters of John Wesley*, 8 vols, London: Epworth, 1931.

Tripp, D. H., *The Renewal of the Covenant in the Methodist Tradition*, London: Epworth, 1969

Tyerman, L., *The Life and Times of the Rev. John Wesley M.A., founder of the Methodists*, 3 vols, London: Hodder and Stoughton, 2nd edn, 1871–6.

Vickers, J. (ed.), *A Dictionary of Methodism in Britain and Ireland*, London,: Epworth, 2000.

Wainwright, G., *The Ecumenical Moment: Crisis and Opportunity for the Church*, Grand Rapids: Eerdmans, 1983.

Wesley, John, *Works of Rev. John Wesley*, ed. A. Outler, 13 vols, Nashville: Abingdon, 1986.

Williams, C., *John Wesley's Theology Today*, London: Epworth, 1960.

Particular works on the Wesleys and the eighteenth-century background

Baker, F., *John Wesley and the Church of England*, London: Epworth, 1970,

Bowmer, J., *Sacrament of the Lord's Supper in Early Methodism*, London: Dacre, 1951.

Butler, D., *Methodists and Papists*, London: Darton, Longman and Todd, 1995.

Campbell, T., *John Wesley and Christian Antiquity: Religious Vision and Cultural Change*, Nashville: Abingdon, 1991.

Eli, R. G., *Social Holiness: John Wesley's Thinking on Christian Community and Its Relationship to the Social Order*, New York: Peter Lang, 1993.

Hunter, F. *John Wesley and the Coming Comprehensive Church*, London: Epworth, 1968.

Lawson, Albert Brown, *John Wesley and the Christian Ministry: The Sources and Development of His Opinions and Practice*, London: SPCK, 1963.

Thompson, E. W., *Wesley, Apostolic Man*, London: Epworth, 1957.

Watson, D. Lowes, *The Early Methodist Class Meeting, Its Origins and Significance*, Nashville: Discipleship Resources, 1985.

Works on nineteenth- and twentieth-century Methodism

Batty, M., *Stages in the Development and Control of Wesleyan Lay Leadership 1791–1878*, Peterborough: Methodist Publishing House, 1992.

Baxter, M., *Memorials of the United Methodist Free Churches*, London: W. Reed, Hamilton, Adams & Co., 1865.

Beckerlegge, Oliver Aveyard, *The United Methodist Free Churches: A Study in Freedom*, London: Epworth, 1957.

Bowmer J. C., *Pastor and People: A Study of Church and Ministry in Wesleyan Methodism from the Death of John Wesley (1791) to the Death of Jabez Bunting (1858)*, London: Epworth, 1975.

Brake, G. Thompson, *Policy and Politics in British Methodism, 1932–1982*, London: Edsall, 1984.

Carter, D., *James Rigg*, Peterborough: Foundery Press, 1994.

Currie, R., *Methodism Divided: A Study in the Sociology of Ecumenicalism*, London: Faber and Faber, 1968.

Davies, R. E. (ed.), *John Scott Lidgett: A Symposium*, London: Epworth, 1957.

Eayrs, G., *British Methodism as It Was, as It Is, and as It Will Be: A Popular Handbook and History to Help Methodist Union*, London: Henry Hooks, 1909.

Hughes, D., *The Life of Hugh Price Hughes*, London: Hodder and Stoughton, 1904.

Jackson, T., *Recollections of My Own Life and Times*, London: Wesleyan Conference Office, 1873.

Kent, J., *Jabez Bunting, the Last Wesleyan*, London: Epworth, 1955.

Methodism in 1879: Impressions of the Wesleyan Church and its Ministers, London: Haughton & Co., 1879.

Oldstone-Moore, C., *Hugh Price Hughes*, Cardiff: University of Wales Press, 1999.

Turner, J. M., *Conflict and Reconciliation: Studies in Methodism and Ecumenism in England, 1740–1982*, London: Epworth, 1985

Turner, J. M., *Modern Methodism in England 1932–1998*, London: Epworth, 1998.

Wakefield, G., *Robert Newton Flew*, London: Epworth, 1969

Ward, W. R. (ed.), *The Early Correspondence of Jabez Bunting 1820–1829*, London: Royal Historical Society, 1972

Ward, W. R., *Religion and Society in England, 1790–1850*, London: Batsford, 1972.

Wilkinson, J. T., *Arthur Samuel Peake: A Biography*, London: Epworth, 1971.

Wilkinson, J. T., *Hugh Bourne*, London: Epworth, 1952.

Works of individual Methodist ecclesiologists and official Methodist doctrinal statements

Barrett, A., *An Essay on the Pastoral Office*, London: John Mason, 1839.

Barrett, A., *The Ministry and Polity of the Christian Church*, London: John Mason, 1854.

Barrett, A., *Pastoral Addresses: Adapted for Retirement and the Closet*, 2 vols, London: John Mason, 1849

Beet, J. A., *The Church and the Sacraments*, London: Hodder and Stoughton, 1907.

Beet, J. A., *A Manual of Theology*, London: Hodder and Stoughton, 1907.

Benson, J., *An Apology for the people called Methodists*, London: Cordeux, 1812.

Bett, H., *The Spirit of Methodism*, London: Epworth, 1937.

Bolton, A. J., *The Other Side*, Peterborough: WMHS Publications, 1994.

Book of Offices, London: Methodist Publishing House, 1936.

Called To Love and Praise: A Methodist Conference Statement on the Church, Peterborough: Methodist Publishing House, 1999.

Christophers, S. W., *The Class Meeting in relation to the discipline and success of Methodism*, London: Wesleyan Conference Office, 1873.

The Constitutional Practice and Discipline of the Methodist Church, Peterborough: Methodist Publishing House, 1999.

Dale, R.W., *The Evangelical Revival and other sermons*, London: Hodder and Stoughton, 1880.

Davison, L., *Sender and Sent: A Study in Mission*, London: Epworth, 1969.

Dixon, J., *Methodism in its Origin, Economy and Present Position*, London: John Mason, 1843.

Findlay, G. G., *The Church of Christ as set forth in the New Testament*, London: C. H. Kelly, 1893.

Findlay, G. G., *The Epistle to the Ephesians*, London: Hodder and Stoughton, 1888.

Flew, R. N., *Jesus and His Church*, London: Epworth, 1938.

Gregory, B., *A Handbook of Scriptural Church Principles*, 2 vols, London: Wesleyan Conference Office, 1888.

Gregory, B., *The Holy Catholic Church, the Communion of Saints*, London, 1873.

Gregory, B., *Sermons, Addresses and Pastoral Letters*, London: Wesleyan Conference Office, 1881.

Hughes, H. M., *Christian Foundations*, London: Epworth, 1927.

Isaac, Daniel, *The Rules of the Protestant Methodists brought to the test of the Scriptures*, Leeds: Barr, 1830.

Jackson, T., *Christian Presbyters, their office, duties and reward*, London: John Mason, 1850.

Jackson, T., *Wesleyan Methodism, a revival of Apostolic Christianity*, London: John Mason, 1839.

Kirkpatrick, D. (ed.), *The Doctrine of the Church*, London: Epworth, 1964.

Kissack, R., *Church or No Church: A Study of the Development of the Concept of Church in British Methodism*, London: Epworth, 1964.

Lidgett, J. S., *The Apostolic Ministry, Sermons and Addresses*, London: Robert Culley, 1910

Lidgett, J. S., *Fatherhood of God*, Edinburgh: T. & T. Clark, 1902.

Lidgett, J. S., *God, Christ and the Church*, London: Hodder and Stoughton, 1927.

Lidgett, J. S., *God in Christ Jesus*, London: Epworth, 1915.

Luscombe, P., and E. Shreeve (eds), *What Is a Minister*, London: Epworth, 2002.

Methodist Service Book, London: Methodist Publishing House, 1975.

Packer, J. (ed.), *The Centenary of the Methodist New Connexion*, London: G. Burroughs, 1897.

Pope, W. B., *A Compendium of Christian Theology*, 3 vols, London: Wesleyan Conference Office, 2nd edn rev. and enlarged, 1880.

Quick, W. A., *Methodism, a Parallel*, London: T. Woolmer, 1889.

Rigg, J. H., *A Comparative View of Church Organisations, Primitive and Protestant. With a supplement on Methodist secessions and Methodist union*, London: Charles Kelly, 3rd edn, 1897.

Rigg, J. H., *The Connexional Economy of Wesleyan Methodism in its Ecclesiastical and Spiritual Aspects*, London: Wesleyan Conference Office, 1852/1878.

Rigg, J. H., *Essays for the Times on ecclesiastical and social subjects*, London: Elliott Stock, 1866

Rigg, J. H., *Jabez Bunting, a Great Methodist Leader*, London: Kelly, 1905.

Rigg, J. H., *The Methodist Class Meeting*, London, 1865.

Rigg, J. H., *The Relations of John Wesley and of Wesleyan Methodism to the Church of England, Investigated and Determined*, London: Longmans, Green and Co., 1868.

Shrewsbury, W. J., *An Essay on the Scriptural Character of the Wesleyan Methodist Economy*, London: Renshaw and Kirkman, 1840.

Simon, J. S., *A Summary of Methodist Law and Discipline*, London: Methodist Publishing House, 5th edn, rev. to the Conference of 1923 by John Elsworth, 1924.

Slater, W. F., *Methodism in the Light of the Early Church*, London: T. Woolmer, 1885.

Statements and Reports of the Methodist Church on Faith and Order, vol. 1, 1933–1983, Peterborough: Methodist Publishing House, 1984.

Statements and Reports of the Methodist Church on Faith and Order, vol. 2, 1984–2000, Peterborough: Methodist Publishing House, 2000.

Watson, R., *Theological Institutes*, 3 vols, London: John Mason, 1828; also in *Works of Richard Watson*, 12 vols, London: John Mason, 1830, vols 10–12.

Wainwright, G., *Methodists in Dialog*, Nashville: Kingswood, 1995.

Other books cited

Abbott, W. M. (ed.), *Documents of Vatican II*, London and Dublin: Geoffrey Chapman, 1966.

An Anglican–Methodist Covenant: Common Statement of the Formal Con-

versations between the Methodist Church of Great Britain and the Church of England, Peterborough: Methodist Publishing House/ London: Church House Publishing, 2001.

Baptism, Eucharist and Ministry, Report on the Process and Responses, Faith and Order Paper, 149, Geneva: WCC, 1990.

Bell, G. K. A. (ed.), *Documents on Christian Unity 1920–30*, 2 vols in 1, London: Oxford University Press, 2nd edn, 1930.

Best, T., and G. Gassmann, *On the Way to Fuller Koinonia*, Faith and Order Paper 166, Geneva: WCC, 1994.

Bishops in Communion: Collegiality in the Service of the Koinonia of the Church, London: Church House Publishing, 2000.

Called to Witness and Service: The Reuilly Common Statement, London, Church House Publishing, 1999.

Churches Together in England, *Baptism and Church Membership (with Particular Reference to Local Ecumenical Partnerships)*, London: CTE, 1997.

Commitment to Mission and Unity, London: Church House Publishing/ Peterborough: Methodist Publishing House, 1996.

Conversations on the Way to Unity: The Report of the Informal Conversations between the Church of England, the Methodist Church and the United Reformed Church, London: United Reformed Church, 2001.

Dunn, James D. G., *Unity and Diversity in the New Testament*, London: SCM Press, 1977.

Gros, J., H. Meyer and W. Rusch, *Growth in Agreement II: Reports and Agreed Statements of Ecumenical Conversations on a World Level*, Geneva: WCC/Grand Rapids: Eerdmans, 2000.

John Paul II, *Ut Unum Sint*, London: CTS, 1995.

Kinnamon, M., and B. Cope, *The Ecumenical Movement: An Anthology of Texts*, Geneva: WCC, 1997.

McAdoo, H. R., and A. Clark, *The Anglican–Roman Catholic International Commission: The Final Report*, London: SPCK/CTS, 1982.

MacKenzie, K. (ed.), *Union of Christendom*, London: SPCK, 1938.

Meyer, H., and L. Vischer (eds), *Growth in Agreement: Reports and Agreed Statements of Ecumenical Conversations on a World Level*, Geneva: WCC/New York: Paulist, 1984.

Mohler, J. A., *De l'unité de l'église ou du principe du catholicisme*, Brussels, 1839.

Nunn, R., *This Growing Unity*, London: Churches Together in England, 1995.

On the Way to Visible Unity: The Meissen Common Statement, 1988, London: Board of Mission and Unity, Church House Publishing, 1988.

Rigal, Jean, *L'ecclesiologie de communion*, Paris: Editions du Cerf, 1997.

Schweizer, E., *Church Order in the New Testament* (ET), London: SCM Press, 1961.

Sesboue, B., *Pour une theologie oecumenique*, Paris: Editions du Cerf, 1990.

Speaking the Truth in Love: Teaching Authority among Catholics and Methodists, report of the Joint Commission for Dialogue between the Roman Catholic Church and the World Methodist Council, Lake Junaluska: World Methodist Council, 2001

Thunberg, L., *Man and the Cosmos*, New York: St Vladimir's, 1985.

Thurian, M. (ed.), *Churches Respond to BEM*, 6 vols, Geneva: WCC, 1986.

Thurian, M., *The Eucharistic Memorial* (ET), London: Lutterworth, 1961.

Tillard, J.-M., *L'église locale*, Paris: Editions du Cerf, 1995.

Together in Mission and Ministry: The Porvoo Common Statement with Essays on Church and Ministry in Northern Europe. Converstations between the British and Irish Anglican Churches and the Nordic and Baltic Lutheran Churches, London: Church House Publishing, 1993.

Zizioulas, J., *Being as Communion: Studies in Personhood and the Church*, London: Darton, Longman and Todd, 1985.

Articles cited

Beck, B., 'Some Reflections on Connexionalism', *Epworth Review*, 18 , 2 (1991), pp. 48–59, and 3, pp. 43–50.

Carter, D., 'Church and Praise in the Hymnody of the Wesleys', *Sobornost*, NS 18, 1 (1996), pp. 30–47.

Carter, D., 'Joseph Agar Beet and the Eschatological Crisis', *Proceedings of the Wesley Historical Society*, 51, 6 (1998), pp. 197–216.

Carter, D., 'A Methodist Reaction to *Ut Unum Sint*', *One in Christ*, 33, 2 (1997), pp. 125–37.

Carter, D., 'Pastoral Office or Sacrificing Priesthood: Towards Reconciliation in Concepts of Presbyteral/Episcopal Ministry', *Methodist Sacramental Fellowship Bulletin*, 127 (1998), pp. 31–47.

Carter, D., 'Speaking the Truth in Love', *One in Christ*, 37, 1 (2002), pp. 73–82.

Harrison, A. W., 'Methodist Churchmanship', *London and Holborn Quarterly Review* (1938), pp. 193–6.

Lofthouse, W. F., 'The Possibility of a United Christendom from the Standpoint of Methodism', in MacKenzie (ed.), *Union of Christendom*, pp. 479–502 (493).

Longbottom, W., 'The Relation of the Methodist New Connexion to other Methodist Churches', in Packer (ed.), *Centenary of the Methodist New Connexion*, pp. 179–229.

Macquiban, T., with additional comment by Rupert Hoare, Michael Townsend and Reg Ward, 'Does Methodism Matter Enough?', *Epworth Review*, 23, 2 (1996), pp. 67–80.

Orcibal, J., 'The Theological Originality of John Wesley and Continental Spirituality', in Davies and Rupp (eds), *History*, vol. 1, pp. 81–119.

Rider, T., ''The Spiritual Life and Aims of the MNC', in Packer (ed.), *Centenary of the Methodist New Connexion*, pp. 230–67.

Robbins, B., and D. Carter, 'Connexionalism and Koinonia: A Wesleyan Contribution to Ecclesiology', *One in Christ*, 34, 4 (1998), pp. 320–36.

Tavard, G., 'Tradition as Koinonia in Historical Perspective', *One in Christ*, 24, 2 (1988), pp. 97–111.

Tavard, G., 'The Dialogue between Methodists and Catholics', *One in Christ*, 30, 2 (1994), pp. 176–83.

Tillard, Jean-Marie, 'Faith, the Believer and the Church', *One in Christ*, 30, 3 (1994), pp. 216–28.

Townsend, W. J., 'Church Principles and Order of the MNC', in Packer (ed.), *Centenary of the Methodist New Connexion*, pp. 1–69.

Turberfield, Alan, 'A Critical Appraisal of John Scott Lidgett', Oxford D.Phil. thesis, 1998.

Walsh, J., 'Methodism at the End of the Eighteenth Century', in Davies and Rupp (eds), *History*, vol. 1, pp. 275–316.

Wellings, Martin, 'Making Haste Slowly: The Campaign for Lay Representation in the Wesleyan Conference 1871–81', *Procedings of the Wesley Historical Society*, 53, 2 (2001), pp. 25–37.

Index

diversity, in church order in New
  Testament 114–15
  internal Methodist 121
  legitimate in order 112
  unity in reconciled 117
divine revelation recorded in Scripture
  75, 110–11
Dixon, J. 34
doctrinal standards, Methodist 73–5
doctrine, link with experience/
  fellowship 61
Dunn, J. 114

Eayrs, G. 72–3
ecclesiology, 'independent', 30, 152
  of non-Wesleyan Methodists 63–7
  trinitarian 112–13
Ecumenical Movement 70, 90, 98, 100
ecumenism 70, 83, 108–9, 118
  spiritual 53
eldership 63
Eli, G. 9–11
episcopacy 47, 61, 83, 84, 97, 99,
  128, 135, 140–1, 145–7
  1981 statement 140–1
episcopal ministry 139, 141
episcopal succession 115–16, 147
  gift of 133
  sign of 24–5, 39, 115–16, 146, 152
episcopate (historic) 29, 57, 97, 140
episkope/oversight 15–16, 31, 41, 62,
  121, 128, 139, 145–7, 154
  mutual ministerial 41–2, 50, 62
Episkope and Episcopacy (reports on)
  128, 145–6
Ephesians, Letter to 56, 78–80, 90–1,
  105
Establishment, A. S. Peake's attitude to
  99
  Wesleyan attitude 29, 51–4
Eucharist/Lord's Supper 76, 87–8,
  103, 116, 126
  lay presidency at 124
eucharistic ecclesiology 116
evangelical conversion (Wesley's) 7
evangelical experimentalism 33, 58, 61
evangelism 28, 32, 34, 81, 104, 118
experience 5, 11, 58, 61, 104, 111

Faith and Order Committee 99,
  109–10, 147
Faith and Order Conference, Lausanne
  (1927) 99; Edinburgh (1937) 99;
  Montreal (1963) 110, 118
Fatherhood of God 90, 93
fellowship 1, 3, 9, 22, 34, 37–8,
  58–61, 64, 71, 94, 104, 152
Findlay, G. 77–81, 85–7, 102, 104
Fletcher of Madeley 25
Flew, R. N. 68, 70, 85–6, 100–1
foretaste, Church as foretaste of
  Kingdom 113, 118
Free Churches 69, 82–4, 98, 107–8
full connexion, reception into 41, 137
functional/ontological understanding of
  ordination 7, 125–6, 136, 143

Great Tradition 120
Gregory, B. xi, xii, 31, 33, 35–40,
  43–6, 47–50, 51–6, 58–9, 68,
  77, 85, 87, 91, 100, 104, 108,
  115–16, 137, 150, 152, 154
golden mean in ecclesiology 60–2
Grindelwald Conferences 82

Harrison, A. W. 69–70
Heitzenrater, R. 1
holiness (scriptural), 5, 11–13, 56, 64,
  73–5, 83, 97, 115, 131
  social 10, 103
Holy Spirit 12, 22, 36–9, 44, 52, 76,
  81, 84, 86, 91–2, 96, 98, 102–3,
  105, 113, 142, 148, 150, 154
Hughes, M. 70
Hughes, H. P. 68, 70–1, 81–5, 87
Hunter, F. 6
hymn books 120–1
hymns 4, 19–23

inculturation 119
indefectibility of Church 116
independency 61–2, 73, 128
Independent Methodists 30
Independents/Congregationalists 27,
  30, 40
infallibility 87, 111, 148
interdependence 48, 150